INTRODUCTION

The electrician and the plumber, two subcontractors on a large construction project, worked side-by-side.

"Positive with positive, negative with negative," the plumber said. "Don't let the hot wire touch the ground wire, that is all that you need to know about electricity. Anyone can do it."

The electrician continued his work in silence.

"I mean, really all you have to do is line the same colored wires up. There is really nothing to it," the plumber continued. "Unless you are color blind, anyone can do it."

The plumber continued in this vein for some time, but the electrician ignored him, focusing instead on his work.

After several minutes of this, the electrician slipped his tools into his pouch and pushed his glasses up his nose.

"The way I see it, crap flows downhill." He said, turning to the plumber.
"Excuse me?" The plumber replied.
"Crap runs downhill. That is all you need to know to be a plumber. I figure it is even less complicated than being an electrician."

That story centers around a very good friend of my dad's. He is a man who had earned his professional respect and admiration, something that he did not hand out carelessly.

As an HR Professional, I have run into my share of non-HR folk who, much like the plumber, see simplicity in what I do and assume that anyone can do it. Instead of connecting the correct wires though, the statement usually sounds something like: "I could do HR. I mean I am good with people." What they don't realize is that most Human Resources people, and by most, I mean me, get their fill of people by the end of the day because people are tiresome.

But they are also necessary.

For all the talk of AI and robots taking over our jobs, as long as there are people doing some type of work, and there are leaders leading them, you are going to have Humans who are Resources for your organization.

HR is a pull activity - meaning that you have to pull people to what they need to do, as opposed to pushing them. You may be able to get away with pushing for a while but eventually, it will catch up to you. Eventually, you will make a call that isn't ideal and your support network will scatter like a school of spooked fish. You can call yourself a Business Partner, but at the end of the day, you are little more than an enforcer of rules you made up in a vacuum.

So, what exactly is Human Resources, and what does it take to be successful in it? Most business leaders would say you need four ingredients: (1) The ability to get along with people, (2) a general understanding of employment law, (3) knowledge of the organization's policies and procedures, and (4) an understanding of best practices. I am not going to dispute any of this, because it's all true, but HR is a lot more. It is also:

- Dispute mediation
- Power without position
- Politics
- Leadership
- Passion for the success of the organization, and
- The knowledge that your organization cannot maximize its potential without its people being on board.

So, from my perspective, a successful Human Resource Professional:

Knows their stuff

They know the laws that are pertinent to the people in their particular organization. This doesn't mean that they are attorneys, but they do know what is, and what is not, legal, and they know when to call for help.

Is a leader

This doesn't mean that they sit at a polished oak table, surrounded by people whose titles start with Chief. As in Chief Executive Officer, Chief Operations Officer, Chief Financial Officer, Chief Information Officer, Chief Bottle Washer... They are leaders because they know their stuff, they show integrity in their dealings, and they treat people - ALL PEOPLE - with respect while never losing sight of the organization.

Knows the business

It only stands to reason that to be successful, no, to simply survive, HR Pros need to understand the business they are working in. You don't need to know all the intricate details. I don't think an HR Pro necessarily needs to know how to code in order to support a software shop, but they do need a fundamental understanding of the business and what constitutes a decent Software Developer, Network Engineer, etc. How can you possibly expect to recruit for positions you do not know anything about? How can you address challenges when you do not understand why these are challenges in the first place? How can you develop effective policies that further your organization's goals when you do not understand what the organization's goals really are, or why the organization even has them as goals in the first place?

So, if you are in HR, you need to:

- Ask (lots and lots of) questions

- Get your hands dirty
- Put in the hours
- Do the work when (and where) the work gets done
- Know the industry
- Etc., etc., etc…

Of course, it also helps to like people

I know what I said at the beginning of this rant about liking people, and I also know that at the end of the day I have had my fill of people. At the same time, I know if I had a job where I didn't actually interact with people on a regular basis, I would lose my mind. I think that can be said for a lot of people, though not just those of us who have chosen a career that is centered around the unwashed masses.

So, what about bad HR people?

To fully understand how to be successful it is equally important to look at what to avoid, so without further ado, I give you my short list of big things that make for a less than stellar HR practitioner. They:

- Are hung up on titles.
- Love to strategize, but their track records for execution are spotty at best.
- Like meetings. Lots and lots of meetings (hint: it makes them feel important).
- Are inflexible to the business, usually hiding safely behind their black and white, clear cut policies.
- Operate in a silo, assessing risk without considering the risk of not taking care of the business.
- Dictate **a lot** more than they collaborate.
- Like to spout off legal jargon and important sounding HR phrases.

So, what does all of this have to do with you, gentle reader? Well, with very, very, very few exceptions I would venture to guess that you work with, around, above and, for people. Therefore, what follows is a compilation of entries from my blog: HR for (Y')all (hrforyall.com), grouped by topic and updated when needed. The purpose of the blog, and now this book, is to demystify the field of HR for everyone because I believe that we are **all** in the business of Human Resources.

I would love to hear from you. Drop me a line at jim@hrforyall.com, or connect with me on Twitter: @cyberperk.

SECTION 1
My thoughts on HR

SO, TELL ME AGAIN, WHAT EXACTLY DO YOU DO?

Many moons ago I worked as a field HR Rep for a chain of retail stores, which is to say I spent a lot of time walking around and talking to people. We didn't have a designated HR Representative at each store, so a big part of my job was getting in front of employees and letting them know who I was, what I did, and then telling them to give me a call if they ever had any questions or needed anything. "HR Liaison" is how they phrased it in the job description, but it was really an inside sales gig and like a lot of salespeople, I used my business cards as a sort of ice breaker. A sample (and regular) interaction often looked something like:

Me: "Hi, (looking at the employee's name tag) Ralph. My name is Jim Perkins."
Ralph: "OK."
Me: (Handing Ralph my business card) "I work in Human Resources and thought I would…"
Ralph: (Looking at my business card) "So what exactly is a Human Resources (insert title at that moment) anyway?"

It was at this point that my whole speech would be derailed as I made a usually futile attempt to explain what I did. By the time I was finished, the employee would give me a dismissive nod before pretending to be called over to help a customer.

This is not limited to retail, though. I have worked in a number of different industries besides retail - manufacturing, design, distribution, consulting - and while it is perhaps not as blatant as the 18-year old who really just wants me to get out of his way so he can get the shoe display straightened before he goes on his break; I run into people all the time, both socially and professionally, who don't have a clue as to what HR is. It is for this reason I present the following diagram:

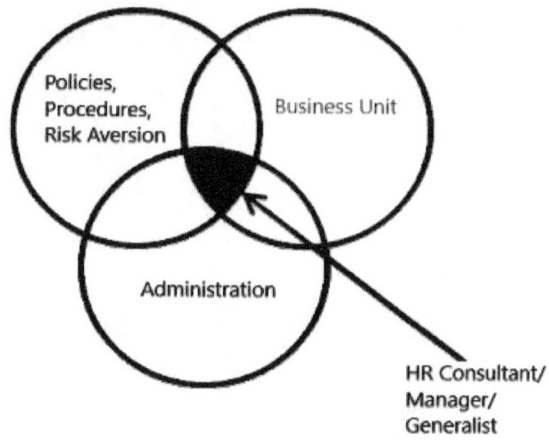

As you can see, there are three circles that intersect:

1. Policies, Procedures, and Risk Aversion
2. Business Unit
3. Administration

The intersection is where your HR Representative falls. Depending on your company or organization, this person may be called an HR Manager, HR Generalist, HR Director, HR Consultant, etc. the title doesn't really matter, what does matter is what this role entails. It is the unique balance between the business unit or the company, the administrative function or the paperwork aspect, and the policies, procedures and other areas, whose goal is to minimize risk to the organization. The trick is to make sure that you maintain the right amount of balance. Try to spend too much time on the policies and procedures side, for instance, and you end up neglecting the business and the administrative duties.

Spend too much time on admin and working with the business, and you end up missing the high-level view that is needed to ensure you have effective policies and procedures in place. In other words, when this gets out of balance, HR's effectiveness usually goes down.

THE LOTTERY

As I write this, the Powerball is at a historic $800 million which is, of course, a WHOLE lot of dough, and as you might expect, you can't turn on the radio, the TV, open your web browser, talk to your neighbor, or do pretty much anything else without hearing about what people are going to do if they win.

First up, let me come clean: I don't play the lottery. It isn't on any kind of moral grounds, I am just cheap. Sure, it's a couple of bucks, but the odds (292.2 million to 1) are that I'm going to be out those couple of bucks. However, the fact that I normally don't play doesn't mean I haven't caught myself daydreaming about what it would be like to win. I may be cheap but I'm also human, and so I have thought of some creative things I could do with that kind of money – a new pair of hiking boots and an Apple Watch are two things that spring to mind immediately (I'm cheap, remember?) Anyway, this brings me to the point of today's entry:

What would **you** do if you won the lottery?

In HR we often use it as a way to sell succession planning. A common phrase goes something like this: "we need to have a succession plan in place in the event that you win the lottery." It sounds better than: "we need to have a succession plan in place in the event you quit, are fired, or die." We choose the first option, even though statistically speaking the odds are much higher that the manager will get another offer closer to their house with better insurance, or get caught embezzling funds. I know, there are those pesky odds again...

But I digress.

So, what *would* you do if you won the lottery? Is it that different from what you are doing now? For me, it's not. I would continue working (with the only difference being I would drive to work in a different Ferrari for each day of the week and take my vacation on my own private island), because I do what I do because I enjoy it. Sure, I enjoy some days more than others, but I do genuinely enjoy it and simply can't see myself sitting at home indefinitely; I would need something to do and my hobbies just aren't that interesting.

But what if you are not in the same place as I am? What if you are one of those people who, should you win the lottery, would just not show back up for work? If that is you, think about what you would do if you did win the lottery, and begin moving towards that goal. If you would genuinely stay home and not do anything, that's OK, but my advice would be to max out your 401(k) because the odds are a lot better.

YOU CAN'T SPELL CULTURE WITHOUT CULT

In HR we love to talk about culture. When things are going well, we cite the organization's culture. When things are not going so great, we are quick to blame the organization's culture. Churning out great products or services? You must have a *culture that values innovation*. Turnover too high? It's *difficult finding a cultural fit*.

But what is culture, really? And how do you go about changing it?

Let's start off by pointing out that it isn't easy because the organization's culture starts with the organization's leadership. The top brass hires people, and then those people hire people. Then those people hire people, and so on, with each hire carrying a little bit of cultural DNA from the person who hired them. Sure, people leave; even the top brass "goes on to pursue other opportunities," but unless the entire organization was to somehow do a complete 100% turnover of personnel overnight, the DNA will stick around.

If the top brass' corporate culture DNA is trickling through the rest of the organization, they had better be careful or their bad genes may work their way into the mix as well. Maybe they have a gene for infighting. Or a gene for valuing "yes-men" and "yes-women." Maybe they have the "I am the CBW (Chief Bottle Washer), and therefore am to be revered, gene." All of these things lead to like-minded individuals who perpetuate into a culture, much the same way as a cult does.

What happens when someone joins a cult but decides it isn't for them? They leave (or at least try to), and then star in Lifetime Original movies. This really isn't that different from corporate America, sans the late-night television specials (with the possible exception of a few dot coms).

To be fair I think that cults have gotten a bad rap. I mean sure, there is that whole mass-suicide thing, but the people who are running them have to have some leadership qualities - if they didn't, no one would join them.

The bottom line here is this: if you want to make a change to your organization's culture, you need to start with the top leadership. If you are the top leadership, look at who you are hiring and the kinds of people you are surrounding yourself with. Do these people exhibit the behaviors you want? If not, what makes you think the people they hire and surround themselves with will be any different?

If you are not the top brass (or in a position to influence the top brass), all hope isn't lost. If you're wired differently you can push your own DNA mutations into the corporate gene pool. I do believe that culture starts at the top, but I also believe that the organization is an organism, and organisms can, and do, evolve. Be part of that evolution. It won't be easy, but it can be done. Of course, there are other options as well: you can always grab your red solo cup and have yourself some Kool-Aid.

EXCUSE ME, I THINK YOU HAVE MY SEAT

In HR we like to talk about gaining a seat at the table. In fact, I have been to conferences where there were breakout sessions dedicated to this concept, which makes me sad because there are folks who think that they need to go to a conference to learn how to get a seat at the table. I wonder what their post-conference meetings look like.

Business Leader: "How was the conference?"
HR Dork: "It was great! I spent two days learning how to get a seat at the table."

I don't see this meeting ending well, in fact at the bare minimum I see the business leader trimming the learning and development budget for the aforementioned HR Dork.

So, what does this elusive, majestic, table look like?

Let's say your company makes rubber balls. The table is going to be represented by all facets that are responsible for the manufacture, distribution, and sales of said rubber balls. In other words, seated around the table are divisions that represent the manufacturing of the rubber balls, selling or marketing the rubber balls, and the logistics for getting the rubber balls from the company's facilities and warehouses to its customers. There's also the financial aspect: accounting for the money coming in and going out, as well as securing the necessary capital to ensure the company has the money to continue making and selling rubber balls. These are the basics, of course, but there is one underlying factor that fits all this together: people (OK, and rubber balls). The company needs to have the right strategy to get the right people hired into the right roles. They need to ensure that their workforce is functioning at maximum capacity. They need to ensure that they are prepared for contingencies like work stoppages and accidents. They need to make sure that their policies are designed so that the business runs at maximum efficiency while still maintaining the flexibility to adjust if needed. All of this falls on the lap of the seat HR seeks at the table. Is the CFO concerned that her labor costs are too high? Talk to the HR seat holder. Is the 3rd shift difficult to fill and does the COO feel that the schedule could be adjusted to make it easier to find folks? That would be the cool HR person's domain. Is the Marketing Veep rethinking her commission schedule? Hello HR.

The challenge is this: in many instances, the head honchos don't think that way; they don't automatically think of their HR business partner as a partner. They think of HR as a necessary evil, as who they go to when they have a problem, not who they go to ensure they *don't* have a problem in the first place. It isn't the leaders' fault, though. It is HR's. You can't fault leaders for not wanting to work with HR on anything other than problems if that is all HR seems to be good at. "Oh, we've got a problem with this employee, we need to call HR." Yes, that is going to happen, and in many cases, it *needs* to happen, but the breakdown occurs when the problem is given to HR, and us HR Pros don't go back and say "OK, this happened. It has been cleaned up and fixed. Now, what do we need to do to prevent it from happening again?" Notice I didn't say "OK, this happened. It has been cleaned up and fixed, now this is what *you* need to do so that it doesn't happen again." This is not what a partner says, it is not a collaborative statement - it is a directive. It is not someone working *with* you, it is someone *bossing you around*, and nobody likes being bossed around, and they sure don't want to sit at a table with that person.

So, if you are in HR, stop being so dang bossy and look at how to collaborate. As for you non-HR folks, I hope you take away from this little chapter that HR truly can help you run your business more efficiently; though sometimes our egos get in the way. So, do me a favor, the next time your HR person gives you a directive, ask them why. Why are they telling you this is what you have to do? If you get push back, just say "I'm asking as a business partner, I need to understand so I can make the best decision." If you still get flack, that might raise some flags about your HR person, and if it happens enough you are probably justified in not giving this person a seat. That doesn't mean that you don't invite HR to the table, you just find someone who truly belongs there.

SO, YOU WANT TO WORK IN HR...

If you spend any time at all with HR people you will notice two things pretty quickly:

1. There are a lot of other places you would rather be than in a room full of HR people, and
2. There is a high proportion of what I call "accidental HR people."

In fact, I consider myself to be an accidental HR person. To explain, let me give you a brief history of my professional career path.

I graduated from college ready to take on the world, which in my case meant managing a now-defunct auto parts retailer. It took me all of 18 months to realize that was not what I wanted to do until I retired so I got my stock broker's license and set out to become a Financial Advisor. That was fun with the slight issue of pay, or rather the lack thereof, meaning I was paid 100% commission. No salary. After about a month of mailing countless letters, reaching out to dozens of friends and relatives and relentlessly cold-calling the phone book (yes, I actually used a phone book, it was a long time ago), I scored a client and within a couple of weeks received my first check in the mail. It was for $0.63. <u>Sixty-three cents</u>, and yes, it **came in the mail**. True, that was my worst month, but when more than a month of hard work adds up to less money than I could have made recycling aluminum cans, you begin to question your career choices. To add insult to injury I actually received an award - called a "SuperSTARter" - because I was one of the top performing first-year advisors. I remember receiving that award and genuinely feeling sorry for the "average" performers in the group. Needless to say, I decided that another career change was in order. Interestingly, my experience as both a Financial Advisor and retail manager put me in a unique position for a retailer looking to increase their 401(k) participation, especially among their store employees. It was an entry-level position which was perfect for me considering minimum wage would have been a major raise. At any rate, that was the beginning and I haven't looked back since.

So, if I had it to do over would I do anything differently?

Nope.

The fact is my time in retail and financial services/sales taught me a great deal that has helped me in my career to this point. For instance:

1. Just about everything comes down to Customer Service
2. We are all in Sales, and
3. Never pursue a job based solely off of earnings potential. Choose something you love.

I am a better HR practitioner because of these three things, and consider my pre-HR time as my informal education. If you are considering a career change - HR or otherwise - and don't know how to get there, take a look at your current job and what you do, then think of how it can help you succeed in the new venture you are pursuing.

One caveat: assuming you are considering taking a leap into the great wide world of HR, "working with people" doesn't count as HR experience.

So what advice would I give someone looking to make the leap into HR? The most important thing is to be prepared to start at the bottom and then ask a lot of questions. It will likely mean you have to take a pay cut and essentially start over. This is what trips people up more than anything: "I've been working for 20 years, I am not ready to be a file clerk..." I get it. Had I not made a salary that made people from developing countries want to send me money, I would likely have not gotten into HR either. But while I can only speak from personal experience, within 5 years my salary had more than doubled from what I was making when I started my HR journey. Why? Because I was hooked. I loved what I was doing and was passionate about it. Did I have some amazing mentors (and more than just a little luck)? You bet I did, but I also got excited about coming to work every day and you have to try to NOT be successful if you love what you do.

THE HR FOR (Y')ALL 4 QUADRANTS OF HR

Here at the HR for (Y')all headquarters (my kitchen table) and our satellite office (a corner booth at Chipotle), we (meaning me) have been puzzling over the big question that plagues so many HR Pros - how do we become Strategic Partners?

There are a good many HR Professionals out there who think that once they have that coveted seat at the table, the non-strategic work, and more specifically the work that does not directly involve the leadership of the organization, is no longer in their wheelhouse. I have challenges with this line of thinking, though. First off, someone has to handle the keep-the-lights-on stuff. Otherwise, you will find that after you have worked at keeping the regulators and lawyers at bay, you will barely have time to conduct the exit interviews you will be doing. Second, and this is something that so many of us HR geeks simply don't get: you cannot *step* into a strategic partner role. **It has to be earned**. Sure, you may be replacing someone who had achieved that status, and therefore you are elevated into it by default, but it will be short lived if you do not cover the other aspects of HR. So, what I have set out to do is try and uncover the types of work that us HR folk do, and then delve not only into why the work matters, but why it is critical not to neglect any of these areas.

To illustrate, I am attaching a diagram that I am calling the HR for (Y')all Mother of all Matrixes (it's my matrix, so I can call it whatever I want).

BUT, BUT... I'M GOOD WITH PEOPLE!!

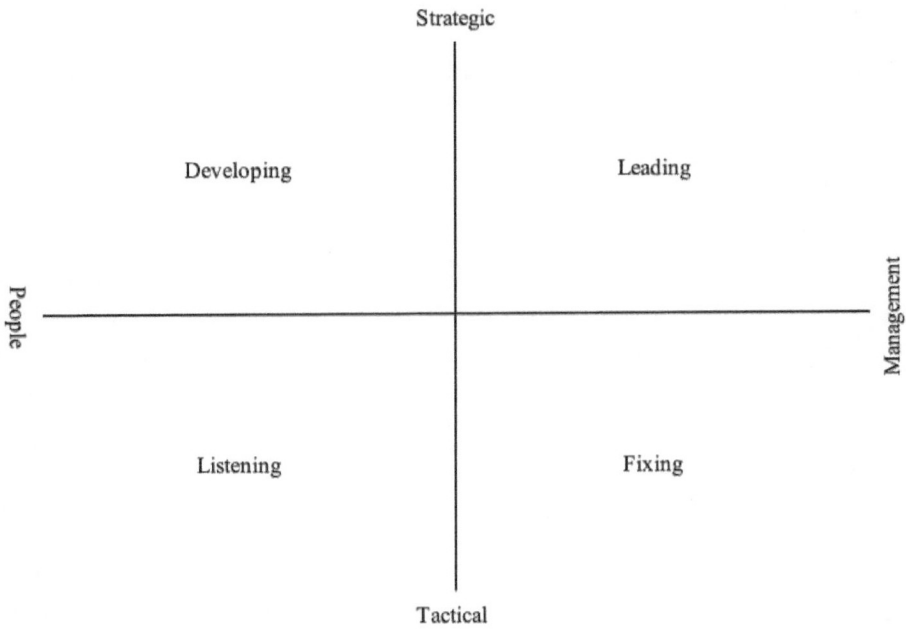

Let's start with the part that no one really wants to talk about: the Tactical/People Quadrant, down in the lower left corner. For whatever reason, this is the piece that everyone wants to skip because it is where a lot of the "Administrative" work lies. Sure, this is the quadrant where employment verifications, chasing down I-9's, and those pesky "my prescription for medical marijuana was a few ounces short" calls to Benefits come in, but it is really the listening quadrant. This is where you build your street cred with the folks you are genuinely supporting; ignore at your own peril.

Move with me now to the upper left corner, the People/Strategic Quadrant. This is where you take your listening and apply it to help the folks you are supporting. To be successful here you need to know what they actually do, which is harder than it sounds. This is knowing their strengths and weaknesses, and then finding how they can leverage them to their best interest. It means career development for the high-potential employees, career maintenance for the good (but not great) ones, and maintaining dignity for the rest when their number is up.

Next, let's zig a little and look at the Tactical/Leadership Quadrant. This is where you execute on the initiatives set out by the leadership of the organization. Oh, and it is where you fix stuff because there are always going to be fires that need to be put out. Don't handle this and you lose street cred as well, only this time it is with the people who can actually fire you. The problem with this quadrant is that it is easy to confuse it with its more mature and buttoned up sibling: the Strategic/Leadership Quadrant. Be careful that you don't confuse "doing something **for** (insert high-ranking executive)" with "doing something **with** (insert high-ranking executive)." It has to get done, but if that is all you do you may find you are not as indispensable as you once thought.

Finally, let's take a look straight up and get to the Strategic/Leadership Quadrant - the golden circle as it were. If you are new to a role and try to jump straight into here without ensuring you are at least covering the other three, you will be dead in the water. Sure the honchos may appreciate the discussion, but when the rubber meets the road on what you all agree needs to get done (Tactical/Leadership), or someone complains because their home loan was rejected on account of the employment verification being too late (Tactical/People), or the high-potentials are leaving and the duds are staying (Strategic/People), the HR for Y'(all) Mother of All Matrices starts to look more like the crosshairs of a rifle scope.

MUSINGS OF A MALE HR PRACTITIONER

I recently signed up for the Society for Human Resources Management's Annual Conference, which is one of - if not the - largest HR Conferences in the country. Every year thousands upon thousands of HR geeks come together from all over the world to hear some of the best and brightest in the field speak, and network. I don't go every year, but when this year's flyer came I signed up. It was only after talking to my wife that I became aware that it started on Father's Day.

Welcome to HR, dude.

I have long observed that HR is a female dominated profession. I truly understand the plight of male nurses because I am in the same boat. I imagine male nurses walking all over conference centers searching for a men's room, only to find that they have all been relabeled women's (and there are STILL lines!). How ironic that the profession that is tasked with ensuring equality has to commandeer restrooms.

So, here's the deal: diversity in the workplace is a good thing. If you don't agree with that, I am not sure why you are reading a book written by anyone in HR (though I thank you all the same - no refunds, sorry). But if diversity is a good thing, why is HR not embracing it within its own ranks? I believe it is because as a profession we have chosen to focus internally, and not made the effort to venture out of our comfort zones. HR people are humans. Sure, our reflections don't always appear in the mirror, and we have that strong aversion to garlic, but we also make the same mistakes as everyone else, one being we hire people that are like us. We do this because it is easier than recruiting folks who don't really "know" HR and then training them in the secret and sacred ways of our profession.

Attentive Reader: "Wait a minute, is he saying HR needs to stop promoting from within?"
Me: "Yep."
Attentive Reader: **GASP**

Those of us who have grown up in HR have tended to stay within our beloved profession and not tried to understand the business that we support. Too many of us don't even attempt to learn the business AT ALL. We don't take time to work within the business or attend meetings in the organization with other departments. We use the same interview questions, whether we are hiring a mechanic or an accountant. We don't walk around where the business gets done because we don't need to know such things because we are HR, dammit! So it shouldn't be a surprise that we have become exactly what we work to prevent elsewhere: a homogenous team of people that all look (and think) alike.

The solution is two-fold and obvious, at least to me.

First, look for people in other places than you normally look to fill talent in the HR ranks, and not just entry-level positions. I have people come to me all the time and tell me they want to get into HR. The problem is, they usually have to start out in entry-level roles. Not that there's anything wrong with that... Oh, wait, there is a lot wrong with that! I know that everyone has to start somewhere, but we're talking about getting experienced professionals who know your business. Doesn't having them start over from scratch kind of defeat the purpose?

This is embedded in our profession, though. Take our certifications for example: in order to sit for most of the ones I am aware of, you need at least two years of exempt-level HR experience.

How are you supposed to get that kind of experience without the certification (I am often asked)? The answer – start out as a clerk (which is usually non-exempt), and work your way up.

Second, HR folks need to spend time with their business units and understand what makes them tick. Stop thinking like an *HR* leader and start thinking like a *business* leader

Work with me here, it ain't that hard.

So, what if you are not in HR (and have no desire to ever be)?

Well, skip the first point (though maybe talk to your HR leadership about their criteria. Ask them "what is an SPHR, PHR, SHRM-SCP or SHRM-CP? How important are those letters, anyway? Is it really more important than having business knowledge? Can you teach them all that HR crap after then learn the workings of the business?"

Second, reach out to your HR rep and invite them to your meetings. Ask them to follow you around and get to know more about what you do. What can it hurt? Will you be better, or worse, off with an HR person who knows more about your business? Be careful how you answer that.

Who knows, maybe someday I can attend a major conference and find a restroom.

One can always dream.

SECTION 2

HR stuff everyone should know, but not everyone understands

AT-WILL EMPLOYMENT

If you are a manager you are likely familiar with the phrase "at-will employment." In fact, it very well may be something that you use when talking with your HR person: "what do you mean I can't fire them? We are an at-will employer!" Or, "I don't even know why I have to go through all this, we are an at-will employment state!"

So, since this is such a popular phrase, I thought it might do all of us some good to brush up on what at-will employment really means.

At-will employment is actually a doctrine that has been around for a while, but it doesn't apply to all employers. For example, the existence of a contract typically voids at-will (think unions). Also, not every state is at-will. If your company <u>is</u> an at-will employer, in an at-will employment state, then essentially your employment can be ended at any time, by either party, i.e. the employee or the employer, for any <u>legal</u> reason, or no reason at all.

The operative word being <u>legal</u>.

In other words, your employer can't end your employment because you are Hispanic – that is illegal (a violation of Title VII) regardless of whether your employment is at-will or not. Generally speaking, your employer cannot fire you just because you are disabled, a woman, pregnant, or too old, and claim "at-will employment."

I can hear you now: "yeah, well if that is the case, they can just tell me that they don't have to give me a reason..." You are correct, that is part of the at-will doctrine: the employer does not have to give a reason, but here's the rub: if you (the employer) did decide to not give a reason for terminating someone, if you are called on the carpet it will be up to you to explain that you, in fact, did not have a reason at all. Meaning you will have to prove that the true reason was not something illegal (like firing the employee because they are an old, disabled, pregnant, Hispanic woman). No court on this planet is going to believe that they did not have any reason at all for firing someone. That defense is just stupid.

Now that being said, if you are fired, the employer still does NOT have to give a reason when they end someone's employment, and they are well within their rights to tell you as much. But (and this is a Sir Mix-a-Lot sized BIG BUT) before you get cocky and start thinking that you automatically have a case, think about your time at said employer:

- Did you do a good job?
- Were you on time?
- Did you do what was asked of you?
- Did they ever have to stop by your cube to "talk about your TPS reports?"

Depending on how you answer these and similar questions, you may want to reconsider whether your time might be better spent looking for other employment as opposed to talking to lawyers.

Now, back to those of you who manage people: stop hiding behind "at-will employment" thinking it will make your job easier because it won't. Eventually, you are going to have to give the reason for letting this employee go, and depending on who that is, you might decide "at-will employment" isn't the panacea that you think it is.

LET'S TALK ABOUT SEX(UAL) HARASSMENT

One part of most HR Pro's lives involve dealing with Sexual Harassment, so it may be a surprise that I have waited this long to talk about it and I am devoting such a short chapter to it. The truth is I don't really feel that there is much to say about it. The way I see sexual harassment, and training for its prevention, is really pretty simple: Don't do it. Sadly, that isn't sufficient in the world that we live in.

I find it to be a sad testament to our society that we have to conduct training to tell people, and yes, I said people - this goes for all sexes - to treat one another with respect. Yet, thanks to a seemingly endless stream of morons, we still need to talk about it.

First up, I want to make clear that this stuff ain't new. Whether it was hunting and gathering ("you know, if you used the smaller fig leaves, I'd be willing to share some of my berries with you,") or in modern work environments with buttons that automatically close office doors, people are people.

So first up let's talk about what happens if you are subjected to harassment. The right thing to do is bring it up within your organization. Maybe you don't have an HR department, or maybe you do but you don't like them *(gasp)*. It doesn't matter because almost everyone has a boss. VPs report to Presidents or CEOs. CEOs report to boards, boards have shareholders. Once you report the behavior it is the organization's responsibility to promptly investigate the concern.

"Psh, forget that," you may be saying. "I'm just going to sue."

Sure, you can do that, but your success rate may not be so hot. First up, you are going to want to find a lawyer. To be more specific, a lawyer who is willing to take your case. Most of the time the lawyer doesn't get paid unless he or she wins your case, so unless they think they have a decent shot at winning, they may decide to pass. Keep in mind if you decided to skip to the front of the line and not at least try to work it out, the lawyer is going to see what the court will see - someone who is not willing to follow the rules. In fact, it is estimated that only between 3 and 6 percent of sexual harassment cases actually go to trial, so there isn't much of an incentive for an attorney to invest a lot of time and money into a case if the odds of even getting to, much less winning at, trial is pretty small.

Does this mean that you don't talk to an attorney if you are subjected to harassment? Of course not. I am just suggesting that this may not be the best course of action for you if you do not give the company a chance to deal with it first. If you cannot work with this person any longer, or you fear for your safety tell them that you need to be separated until the investigation is concluded. And don't forget the three D's: document, document, document.

That said, very few companies want to deal with the cost of defending a sexual harassment claim, regardless of the odds of success. While they can't stop you from filing a lawsuit, they can present evidence that they looked into the allegations and dealt with them appropriately, which is their best defense and likely to be the cheapest way to deal with these types of things.

Now, if you are an employer or boss, here is a short, but if followed, very effective sexual harassment training primer: if you are engaging in this type of behavior, and you will know if you are, **STOP**. This is a job, not a booze cruise. If you are just kidding around, it ain't funny (and I am an expert in what's not funny), so I repeat, **STOP**. Now get back to work.

THESE ARE THE BREAKS

I think it is time we dispel a well-circulated myth around breaks, as in 15-minute, sit in the break room and do nothing breaks (not restroom breaks). I can't believe I actually have to put that caveat in, but I do.

Before we begin, let me preface this by saying that I have been called a lot of ugly names, but a lawyer isn't one of them. So, while I may venture into some legal topics, nothing here is meant to be construed as legal advice.

Alright, now that we have that out of the way, let's talk about breaks. There is a long-held notion that employees are guaranteed, by law, a break after so many hours of work (4 hours seems to be the most common, but it varies). Employees often tell their bosses this and I suppose they say it with such conviction that the manager believes it must be true. This same manager is then truly mind-blown when their HR person tells them, in the most polite, friendly, and non-condescending tone they can muster, that this is not the case.

I can only speculate as to what the cause is, but I suspect that it has something to do with widespread company policies that often get confused for the law of the land. *I worked at Walmart, and they do it, so it must be the law.* (By the way, I have never worked for Walmart, so I am not speaking to their policies.) More speculation: I suspect that companies do this in order to ensure compliance across all their locations. If super hippie liberal state A

(California) has a law that super totally awesome state B (Texas) doesn't have, it is often easier to make a company policy that will keep you out of trouble in state A and apply it nationwide than to try to tailor your policies for each state.

So back to breaks. Let's say you run a single location, do you have to give your employees a break every X hours worked? The standard, HR Magic 8-Ball answer is: "It depends." If we are talking about God's Country (Texas), the answer is, as of this writing, no (barring any municipal laws, of course). You can work your employees as long as you want, so long as you pay them properly. Don't pay them properly, and you are going to find yourself in a very small world of very big hurt. Granted, there are 49 other states in this blessed Union, not to mention individual municipalities that may have different laws (even in the Lone Star State), so for the love of all things holy, chat with your HR Geek or legal counsel before telling someone that the only break they are entitled to is you breaking your foot off in their keister if they don't get back to work. Actually, I would refrain from making that statement regardless of what state you hang your hat in.

One final word: just because you **have** the right, doesn't **make** it right. Treat your employees like sub-humans, and they WILL leave you. Or at least the good ones will, leaving you with a workforce of terrible performers. But hey! At least *they* never take breaks (by the way, that is me being sarcastic).

AND NOW A WORD ABOUT FMLA

If you've been in *any* form of *any* job for *any* length of time there's a good chance you have heard of the Family Medical Leave Act of 1993, better known as FMLA. While almost everyone has heard of it, no one seems to really understand it. Let's try and change that, shall we?

In a nutshell FMLA is job protection - plain, pure and simple. In most instances, it is an unpaid leave, but that doesn't mean you can't get paid while on FMLA. This is because it can be taken along with sick, vacation, PTO short-term disability, or any other kind of paid benefit. However, if you have exhausted, or are otherwise are not eligible for these types of benefits, FMLA in itself will not provide you with a paycheck (at least not as of this writing).

OK, so if you don't get paid, what good is it?

As I said earlier, FMLA is job protection, which ain't a bad thing to have. Sans FMLA, just because you are using sick time or vacation, does not mean that you cannot be fired. Even short-term disability is nothing more than an insurance policy for your lost income, not job protection. Therefore, FMLA is like an umbrella that you tuck all this other stuff under.

So, how do you know if you qualify? Answer a few simple questions:

First, does your employer have 50 or more employees within 75 miles of where you work? This is important because let's say you work for Acme Oil and Gas, a fairly large energy company with 2,000 employees worldwide. So far, so good, except you are stationed at their Notrees, Texas office with one other Acme employee named Bob and a 3-legged dog y'all started feeding. In this case, Acme may still offer you FMLA, or some type of FMLA-like benefit but under the strictest sense of the law, they are not <u>required</u> to do so unless there are other locations within 75 miles of Notrees and the total employee count is at least 50 (3 legged canines don't count).

Second, have you worked for the company for at least 1 year?

And finally, within that 1 year have you worked 1,250 hours?

If you answered yes to all of these questions, congratulations, you are FMLA eligible.

So, what does FMLA cover?

1. Birth or adoption of a child - this is good for either Mom or Dad.
2. You, or an immediate family member, has a serious health condition.
3. Certain situations related to an immediate family member being called up to foreign active duty in the armed forces. By certain situations, I mean things like issues arising due to short-notice deployments, child care, or care for parents of the service member related to the deployment.
4. To care for an immediate family member who has returned from active military service and is undergoing medical treatment.

Does this mean if you are on FMLA that you can't be fired? No. If you were a terrible employee and just happen to go out on FMLA as your boss is getting wise to you, don't think that you can wave the FMLA card and be given some kind of immunity. Yes, your employer will need to be more diligent proving that they are firing you due to something that is *not* FMLA related, which just means that they will just have to *prove* that you suck - they can't expect someone to take their word for it.

THAT S**T AIN'T FAIR

A big part of my job in HR is ensuring that the workplace is fair and everyone feels comfortable at work. This means that sometimes I am brought in as a neutral third party to investigate concerns and get as close to the truth as possible. The thing about investigations is that they are finite, meaning they have an end, with the final result being to bring closure, not just for the organization, but also the person who brought the issue up. For the complainant, closure means that I not only looked into their concern, but I took it, and by extension them, seriously. This gets tricky because, while I make it a point to usually let the person know the issue has been addressed, I also tell them that I can't go into specifics about how it was addressed. As you may imagine, sometimes this can be a tough pill to swallow, because they want to know justice was served! They want revenge!

Telling someone that the issue has been addressed appropriately just doesn't satisfy the blood lust the way telling them exactly what happened, or will happen, to the offending party. To go into lurid details is actually a disservice to everyone involved, though. Trust me, no one is served by hearing all the details about what did or did not happen to Johnny after he made that joke about the hard of hearing genie.

Now, just because this is the right thing to do, doesn't mean that it comes naturally. Truth be told, when I was starting out I struggled with it. I couldn't keep from putting myself in the shoes of the person who had initially come to me. I could see these folks sitting there thinking: "Here's this HR guy sitting across from me, all decked out in his plaid shirt and Dockers, telling me that it has been addressed, and that should it happen again to come and talk to him, but why? What good is it going to do? I just saw Johnny in the lunchroom, walking around like nothing happened! He is still here with his Salisbury steak, Jell-O, and his inappropriate, and not very funny, jokes. So what good did it do for me to go talk to this guy in the first place?"

The thing is I am neutral, and to be neutral I have to be fair, and in order to be fair, I have to treat everyone the same. Johnny screwed up, Johnny has a letter in his file and is on a short leash. In fact, I am fairly certain that Johnny wished the whole thing had never happened. However, to share this is not fair to Johnny. He has been addressed, and to tell the complainant the gory details doesn't do anything but increase unnecessary gossip. So, when I am asked what happened I respond by saying that it has been addressed. If they push, I simply state that out of fairness to Johnny I am not going to go into details. In my experience, the second half of this statement as the desired effect because, even though someone may want to know more, they also know that they might be in Johnny's boat someday and thus will appreciate the same treatment.

So, takeaways:

If you are a manager and you have to address one of your employees, show them the respect everyone deserves and keep the details to a need to know basis: meaning your boss, your HR Rep, and/or whoever your organization dictates. If someone comes to you wanting to know what happened with the issue of fill in the blank, simply reply that it has been addressed. If they push for details, appeal to their sense of fairness. Tell them that if you were in their shoes, you wouldn't share that, so you are simply extending the same courtesy them.

If you are someone who has been wronged and you have gone to HR, please don't hate on them for not giving you a detailed, blow-by-blow account of what happened. They may not give you the fairness speech, but just assume that is the reason for the tight lips.

And if you are Johnny - eat your Salisbury steak and Jell-O and leave the bad jokes to the professionals, and HR writers.

DOCTOR'S NOTE? AIN'T NOBODY GOT TIME FOR THAT!

I am writing this as I recover from an especially tough bout of bronchitis. As I lay on my couch contemplating whether I should go to the doctor and be told that there is nothing she can do for me other than rid my wallet the burden of my co-pay, my mind drifts to that seemingly universal practice of requiring a doctor's note after being out for 3 days, and its origin story.

Where did the so-called 3-day rule come from, and why is it so prevalent? I'm going to be honest and say that I am not 100% sure, though not being sure has never stopped me from speculating. In this case, my bet is that it goes back to the oh-so-ambiguous "serious health condition" piece of the Family Medical Leave Act of 1993. If the Family Medical Leave Act of 1993 sounds familiar, I am proud of you, you are paying attention. If it doesn't sound familiar, BUSTED! You either skipped a chapter or aren't paying attention. Either way: shame, shame, everyone knows your name.

One reason for taking a leave of absence under the FMLA is if you or an immediate family member has a "serious health condition." Since that language is pretty vague, the criteria had to be fine-tuned a bit, a responsibility that first fell to the Department of Labor and then the courts. When all the shouting was over, one definition of sorts arose: if someone is incapacitated for more than 3 days requiring ongoing medical treatment, then they have a serious health condition.

Again, this is speculation on my part, but even if the FMLA isn't the reason for the 3-days-and-I-need-a-doctor's-note rule, it still makes sense that an employer would ask for it. If someone is going to be out for 3 days in a row, their condition may actually be a "serious health condition" and the employer may be obligated to offer additional job protection under the FMLA. If you are the employee, FMLA is a benefit that you may be entitled to and can provide you with an extra layer of job protection, which is not something to be taken lightly. Of course, there are other factors that also determine whether someone is eligible for FMLA (go back a few chapters if you need a refresher).

The bottom line is this: regardless where you fall, employee or employer, if you (or your employee) are out for 3 or more days a doctor's note is good protection for both of you.

Oh, and I am feeling better. Thanks for asking.

LET'S TALK ABOUT MONEY. NOT

The time has come to dispel yet another common myth, one is near and dear to most of our hearts: money, and the myth that you can fire someone for talking about how much money they make. The problem with this logic is talking about money is what is known as a protected activity, and to fire (or discipline) someone for doing it is a violation of the Fair Labor Standards Act, which means yes - you can talk about how much money you make and no you cannot fire or otherwise discipline someone for talking about it. I run into this urban legend all the time, and I can understand why, it just doesn't seem right - that people can sit around and talk about their income and I can't stop them.

Now, that being said, let me put out a little word to the not-so-wise. If, even after reading this, you decide that you still want to go and chat up your co-workers about their pay, all I can say is good luck. I honestly cannot recall a single, solitary situation where this has ended well. Just because you **can** do something doesn't mean you **should**. First off, and this is going to come as a shock, but people lie. Don't believe me? I have a 28-inch waist. That is not true (I have a 30" waist). Ha! Fooled you again!! Second, though you are probably legally within your rights, and your employer can't do anything to you for talking about your pay, that doesn't mean that it will endear you to your boss. Third, and you should have seen this coming, loopholes exist. For instance, some industries and positions are exempt from the can't talk about pay rule. Also, you don't have free reign to go and do this when you should be working, not only is that not cool, it's probably not protected. Finally, if you haven't figured it out yet, I am in Texas, so my experience is primarily related to this great state. Other states, while less civilized in almost every other respect, may have explicit laws around this (and no, I am not just referring to California, though they do come to mind).

So, if you are an employer and have someone who is running their mouth about their dough, it very well may be worth a conversation with them, but be careful. Consult with your HR dude or dudette, your attorney, or both (trust me, it'll be fun) and let them know what is going on. Feel free to let them know that you read this awesome book by this awesome HR guy and you know that you probably can't do anything to them, but at the same time you would like to talk to them and "curb the behavior." HR people and Employment Lawyers love it when you talk dirty like that.

SMELL YOU LATER

Let me take a moment to introduce you to a special kind of employee. For purposes of this chapter let's call him Ivan - Ivan Odor - and Ivan has, well, an odor. Maybe it just popped up, maybe it has been a bit of a problem from the beginning. Maybe you have noticed it on your own, or maybe someone came to you and said something, or maybe you overheard some of your other employees talking about it. It doesn't matter because it's there, and you are aware. Sure, you may be tempted to let it ride; hold your breath and hope for the best as it were. I mean it is a personal matter, so should you even address it at all?

Yes, you should.

All your employees represent your division or department, and more importantly the organization, so you have to hold them accountable for how they present themselves. Also, something like this can cause significant disruption: rumors and gossip, mean pranks, and other petty and childish things that some of your less than ideal employees might decide to cook up.

So, how do you go about addressing this issue? This is deep, so grab a piece of paper and/or a highlighter.

Ready?

You talk to Ivan.

I know that is way out there, but you gotta trust me on this. Talking to your employees is a good thing.

Let him know that you have observed that his personal hygiene is below satisfactory standards. I know that sounds cold and distant, like something that the EPA might say, but it is best to depersonalize this as much as possible. Also, it is very important not to bring anyone else into the conversation. <u>You</u> are the manager, <u>you</u> are the one who observed it, *not* Joe, or Betty. Make sure that he understands that <u>you</u> in no way want to embarrass him, and in fact that this is why <u>you</u> wanted to have the conversation with him. Let him know that <u>you</u> want to get in front of this now in order to minimize distractions in the workplace and avoid any lasting damage to his reputation.

Once you've dropped this on him, Ivan is probably going to be embarrassed. I can hear you asking yourself: "Wow! How does he know these things? It is like he is clairvoyant or something!" To this, I can only reply that I am a professional. At any rate, Ivan will likely apologize and agree to make necessary changes, but when you are dealing with people, things don't always go as we planned. Pride is a powerful thing, and no matter how nicely you tell someone that they stink, sometimes people still take offense to it. If things go down this path it is important to remain focused on your key point, which is to make him aware of the problem and that he needs to address it. If he continues to not see the issue, hold your ground. If, after some time, he still refuses to recognize the issue you may have to expand on the fact that if he doesn't deal with it, it could result in discipline, and even the loss of his job. I would keep this card up your sleeve as long as possible, though. Sometimes telling someone they stink, then following it up immediately with a threat to their job can really put a hurt to someone's feelings. Be patient as long as you can.

Now, there's always a decent chance this is something outside of his control, and by out of his control I mean health-related, not that his woman left him and he doesn't know how to do laundry. If you think this is the case, get your HR guru involved pronto. This isn't to say he gets a free pass to stink up the joint, but you don't want to get you or your company inadvertently committed to something without thinking it all the way through.

I get it, this is touchy and it will likely make you uncomfortable, but to ignore it could be far worse for Ivan: gossip, snickering, alienating him, all the usual Junior High School stuff, which is just going to be a pain in the posterior for you as well. If you talk candidly and give him the opportunity to fix it, you greatly increase your chances of a better outcome for everyone.

IGNORANCE CAN BE CORRECTED, BUT STUPID IS FOREVER

William Shatner was once on a television show called "$@%# my dad says," which was based on a book, which I believe was compiled from a Twitter feed. I never watched the show, but I did flip through the book at a Barnes and Noble once, and have to say that some of the bits I read were pretty funny. Perhaps they resonated with me because I can relate, my dad definitely had his share of colorful sayings. One of these nuggets of wisdom being: "Ignorance can be corrected, but stupid is forever." Perhaps you may have heard this phrase's cousin: "you can't fix stupid." Either way, the man had a point, especially when it comes to employees. By this I mean, are you spending your resources to make someone better that just won't get any better? Are you confusing ignorance for stupidity? Are you trying to fix something that can't be fixed?

Put another way, have you ever had someone that, no matter how hard you tried to coach and guide them, they simply kept going back to their bad behavior or continued making the same mistakes? At some point, you have to decide whether that can be *corrected*, or if it is a *forever thing*. If it is a forever thing, maybe it should be a forever thing somewhere else...

As a side note, when I wrote this original blog post my dad was still spinning words of wisdom. As I revamp this post for another medium (i.e. the book you are now holding), Dad has taken on another medium as well and I miss him daily, along with all the $@%# he used to say.

THE PROBLEM WITH POLICIES AND PROCEDURES

In HR we like our procedures, in fact, probably the only thing we like more than our procedures are our policies. Of course, let's not forget our processes – they are definitely a close third. In fact, you might want to call this the HR Trinity.

Don't get me wrong, it is HR's responsibility to keep the organization out of trouble and one way this is done is by establishing good policies, processes, and procedures. It is also our responsibility to ensure that they are consistently followed. So, what happens when your policies stifle your ability to do business? Or undermine your authority as a manager?

Nevah! You say. That will never happen here!

Oh, but it does...

First up, keep in mind that once a policy is established, you are kinda, sorta bound to it. If you have a policy that says employees cannot be more than 5 minutes late or they are placed on warning, you need to follow that policy, even if you have a star performer whose one fault is he just can't roll in within that 5-minute window. Never mind that he does the work of three other team members - if that is your policy you are going to be hard-pressed not to follow it, even if it means you lose that employee. "Ah, Jim we have to have some leeway..." and I would agree with you, except you have this pesky policy in place. So, if you decide to make this one exception, then word gets out to some of the others who you have fired under this policy, how are you going to defend it? Especially if your star performer happens to be a perfectly healthy white guy who is under 40... and one (or more) of your current or former employees who have been subject to this same policy, well let's just say they don't fit into one of those unprotected classes... I'm going to go out on a limb and say it will be problematic.

So, what's your alternative?

Start by looking at the reason for the policy in the first place. I obviously made up the example earlier, but I have seen some policies that aren't far off from it, especially in the retail and service sectors. In these cases, you have folks who work various shifts and they need to arrive on time so that others can get off without a.) accruing overtime and/or b.) leaving the department or area unattended. These are legitimate business reasons, but are there other tools in your toolbox? Can you cross-train others from different departments to fill in should someone be running a few minutes late, for instance? This isn't to say that you can't address attendance, but perhaps a broad policy of "excessive attendance may result in disciplinary action, up to and including termination" might be more suitable. What is excessive attendance, you ask? It is kind of like the difference between art and pornography - you will know it when you see it.

Another issue I have seen is that policies and procedures are often used as a crutch for a weak manager. It never ceases to amaze me that managers will come together and put a policy or procedure in place to address something that one person is doing within their department. Bob just can't seem to get to work on time, and it is becoming a problem. So, instead of sitting down with Bob and showing him how to set the alarm on his phone, the manager brings everyone together and says that they are implementing a new policy surrounding attendance. Not only does Bob know it is directed at him, so does the rest of the team – which could not only lead to resentment of Bob but also the realization that you are being a chicken and not dealing with the issue head-on.

So, at the end of the day am I suggesting we get rid of policies? Nope. I do work in HR after all and have to show my face to my colleagues. What I am saying, though is give some serious thought before you push for a policy/procedure/whatever. Give some thought as to what you are looking to accomplish and think on whether there is a better solution out there.

THE DARK SIDE OF THE MOON(LIGHTING) POLICY

A friend recently sent me an article detailing things to avoid when considering a new job. As I read it, one thing it listed was moonlighting policies. I found this interesting since I had recently stumbled onto several other articles in the HR press (yes, there is such a thing, stop snickering), that also spoke to these policies and why companies needed to get rid of them.

I have never worked for, or with, a company that either: (a) had a moonlighting policy, or (b) considered having one. So, without the benefit of another perspective, I have never understood the rationale behind such policies in the first place, or at least not the business rationale. For me, the only true benefit is that they give the boss some feeling of authority over his or her subordinates outside of the workplace, but of course no one is going to openly admit that. I don't need any fingers to count how many times a manager has called me and said "I want to implement this policy because I want to control my employees beyond these four walls and beyond their scheduled work shift. It gives my life meaning," but I digress.

Perhaps there are other reasons besides just the boss' need to overcompensate for their general feeling of lack of power outside of work. Perhaps they had an employee who held down a second job and came in tired all the time and it affected their work. In this case, my advice would be to sit down with the employee and let them know that you are paying them to perform a job to a degree of competence, and upon recent review, you have determined that their work is slipping. While you are not entirely sure of the reason, you suspect it may have to do with their side hustle. Go on to tell them that you don't care what they do outside of work (or at least you shouldn't) so long as it doesn't interfere with the job you are paying them to do. However, let them know that if it does impact their work, they may need to make a decision.

That wasn't so hard, was it? What this does is get to the heart of the issue - the performance - and keeps you from looking petty, and who isn't about not looking petty?

I (HEART) ANNUAL REVIEW TIME

As I write this, we are coming up on week three of the new year, which means that I am still writing the wrong date and am breaking the last of my resolutions. I am also entering that time of year commonly known in the HR world as the Seventh Circle of Hell; though everyone else knows it as Performance Review Season.

To recap, Performance Review Season or PRS (which is very close alphabetically to PMS) is when your manager takes that fictional account known as your self-evaluation and reconciles it with their own spotty recollection of your accomplishments for the year and gives you a grade. Unless you work for a dentist or some other sadist, they enjoy this exercise about as much as you do.

So, let me give you some advice on handling this wonderful time of the year:

If you are a manager, own the review. You are writing it and you know you are going to deliver it, so stand behind it. Don't try to pass it off as coming from your boss: "I wanted to give you a higher score but my boss said no." Don't try to blame the company's culture or unwritten policies: "I would have given you a higher score, but the company discourages giving them out." Don't blame HR: "The form that HR gave us doesn't really speak to all the things you are good at, otherwise you would have scored better." By not owning the review, you are saying that you are nothing more than a tool and that the person who is really in charge is above you.

If you are the recipient of the review, own it as well. Take ownership for what you need to improve upon, otherwise, you will never go anywhere. Sure, you walk on water. Sure, the entire organization will collapse without you. Sure, you carry your boss on your shoulders. Sure, you are indispensable... The problem with this is you are the only one who sees it, and unless you are also the one who is making and approving your salary recommendation, and determining what future roles you may be considered for, your personal opinion of yourself doesn't amount to much more than a hill of beans. If there is a disconnect between what you see and what your boss sees, you are going to be at a disadvantage.

Let me be clear here: your review <u>shouldn't</u> come as a surprise. That said, sometimes it does. I am not excusing your manager, but at the end of the day, you are the one who is going to feel it. You are the one who was planning that trip to Aruba based on your expected bonus, only to find that instead, you are going to spend a weekend in the next county at a La Quinta. In other words, the bad news is your review score is probably baked, along with your increase and bonus. Fighting your score is, as Kurt Vonnegut might have said, like trying to stop a glacier.

The good news is you have been given a roadmap, or a plan, or at least a glimpse into what your boss wants from you and what you need to focus on. Maybe the review is focused on how you logged 6 hours of sales calls a week while the expectation was a minimum of 25 hours. Might I suggest you start a call log at the beginning of each week and track your time on calls? Meet with your boss as often as you need to, and always have that sheet in front of you to show her your progress. Then follow up by asking what you are missing.

Now if you will excuse me, I have my performance review in a couple of minutes.

LAWS, POLICIES AND BEST PRACTICES

Before I get started, let me reiterate that I am not a lawyer, nor do I aspire to be one; I don't even want to play one on TV. However, in my profession, it does help to stay up with some legal trends – especially employment law. So, while I am not an attorney, I still like to think of myself as fairly well versed in matters of employment and labor law, which is why it always amuses me when someone comes to me and tells me that "we" (and by "we" I am referring to the employer) cannot do X, Y, or Z because it is "against the law." *Cue Law and Order Theme*

If you have ever stepped foot into a retail store of any size, you have probably found yourself standing in one of a handful of very long checkout lines, while rows of registers sit empty with no cashier. In the retail world, this is known by the managers as "$^%#@! where are all the cashiers!" To further aggravate matters, it is not uncommon in these situations for a cashier who is working the line to look at his or her watch, realize they have been working for 4 hours without a break, shut off their light and direct the line to another register. Their reasoning is "I have been working 4 hours, I am entitled to a break." As discussed earlier, this idea that you are entitled, by Federal law, to a break after 4 hours is a fairly common fallacy, that reaches far beyond retail.

It doesn't seem fair, really. This idea that employees can be required to work as many hours as needed, and not afforded breaks, yet save for a handful of states, there are no laws requiring them. Don't believe me? Google state break laws.

Does this mean that employers should make people work non-stop without a break? Uh, no, and not only because that would be a crummy practice, but also because there are plenty of other places these employees can go to work - or at least the good employees. So just because something isn't legally prohibited doesn't mean it shouldn't be done.

Another example is leaves of absence. There are several legitimate ways to take a legally protected leave of absence, but perhaps the most widely known is FMLA (remember that one?) Granted, not every employer is covered, but this is a pretty broad law and if your company has need for an HR person, chances are its employees qualify under FMLA or, a more lenient state or local equivalent. But what does FMLA cover? Birth or adoption of a child; or to care for yourself, your spouse, parent or child who suffers from a Serious Health Condition, and recently amended to provide for leaves for families with returning service members. So, what if your dog is ill? Sorry, Charlie, that isn't covered under FMLA. Should it be? I honestly don't think so, but I do think that a lot of good will can get behind an employer who gives someone some flexibility if they are dealing with something like this. For example, several years ago I had a Dalmatian who was every bit a part of my family as anyone else. However, after a long life of chasing squirrels and peeing on trees, Pete went on to the great fire hydrant in the sky. That was over 15 years ago, but I still have his picture in my home office. When I lost him, I called to let my boss know I was going to be a little late because I needed to take care of him. She told me to not come in – she didn't tell me to use sick time or vacation, she just told me not to come in and to take the time that I needed, which I did. OK, so maybe this falls more under bereavement, but the bottom line is there isn't a law that entitles me to anything. My boss, and by extension my employer, showed me a level of empathy that I am still grateful for. In other words, sticking strictly to the law isn't always the best practice.

The same goes for policies. No doubt policies are written for the best interest of the company at heart, but there is always something that is not considered; something that goes against the policy in writing, but may not make sense to the company. As an HR practitioner, it is easier to tow the policy line and not waiver (not to mention it usually makes the lawyers happier), but what about the person you are working with? What if they knew that there is a policy in place, but also knew you actively sought out a loophole (or loosely interpreted a policy) to allow for something to happen that you didn't have to? Is that person more or less likely to fire up their computer once they get home (or at work – on your dime) and check Indeed.com?

If you are not an HR person, what is your takeaway? First, don't BS a BSer. Don't tell someone that something is the law unless you are absolutely certain. Instead, make your case from the standpoint of the business. "Look, I know I am not entitled to a break, but the lines seem to be slowing a bit, so I thought I would run up and grab a snack since I am not scheduled for lunch for another two hours." Dog died? Explain that you really hate to miss work, but you just don't know how productive you will be. Hopefully, your manager will understand and have some compassion. If not, they probably aren't the only game in town.

THE EVER-PRESENT, OH-SO-REAL THREAT OF DRUNK TEXTING

The line between our work and personal lives is blurring at a breakneck pace, largely fueled by the practice of BYOD (bring your own device) which started with cellphones and has moved into tablets, laptops, and who knows what else.

Of course, there has always been a tendency for people to use their work machines for personal use, whether it was surfing the internet and paying bills, to the extreme of canceling personal cellphones and landlines and relying exclusively on their work phones. I certainly understand the draw - my pockets get pretty full with all my crap - but there are risks as well.

Case in point, I recently read about a sexual harassment case where an employee received a very odd, but definitely suggestive, text by her boss after hours. While the article didn't state it, it is my well-honed professional opinion that the message in question was, as we say in the HR trade, a drunk text.

I am not here to belabor the ins and outs of the case (the company actually got off on a technicality). Instead, what I want to talk about is the personal/professional line that got blurred when the boss started texting his employee on *her personal phone* from *his personal phone*. The fact that he was (probably) intoxicated leaves me to believe that he had her number in his address book (I can't remember my own phone number when I'm sober...) which brings me to the jist of this: why did he have *her personal phone number* in the address book in *his personal phone*?

Here's a hypothetical: let's say you have been exchanging some steamy texts between a lovely number named Cecilia. Good for you, except when you text Cecil, one of your subordinates who is also in your address book, and tell him that you can't wait to _____ (just let your imagination run wild here), and then you hit send. Maybe you realize what you did or maybe not. Best case scenario you are embarrassed. Worse case... I'll let your imagination run wild on that one too.

You may feel that the headache of having to carry two phones is just not worth it, or maybe your company has a BYOD policy, and it is just unfeasible to NOT keep your addresses where they are easily accessible.

If this is you, I can't suggest enough that you make some work-arounds. Start by looking at your address book app - there is likely a way you can create a separate address book for your work contacts. Or perhaps it is time to consider an app where you get a separate number. Sure, it costs a few bucks, but it may be worth considering. Another simple solution may be to download a separate app for your work stuff, like Outlook. I know there are a number of options out there, but I can speak from personal experience that Outlook does keep everything separate. Maybe it is a little different, and may even take a little getting used to, but it can save you from an embarrassing situation, and that is what I am here for - keeping you from looking like a moron.

You are welcome.

IT'S THE MOST WONDERFUL TIME OF THE YEAR...

I love the holidays. I am probably one of the few HR people who will admit that, but it's true. What's not to love? There is shopping and the lovely crowds of people all filled with the holiday spirit; the weather cools down to a nippy 70 degrees here in Houston, I watch *Love Actually* with my wife, she watches *Die Hard* with me, and we both watch *Elf* with our son - and let's not forget office holiday parties!

Oh wait, I just remembered why HR people hate the holidays...

Everyone has a story about a holiday party going south, and HR people are no exception, though I can honestly say that I have been luckier than most of my colleagues in this regard. That doesn't mean that I don't cringe just a little when I attend these things because, while it is not "work", it is still a "work-sponsored function," meaning that most of the rules still apply.

So here's some quick advice so we can all have a Merry Christmas, Happy Hanukkah, or just enjoy the general season if you don't have a holiday to celebrate, or I missed yours:

Managers: if you see someone getting a little too loose, you've got to reign that in right then, hear me? It doesn't matter if it's a group dinner at Chili's and you haven't gotten past the chips and queso, your manager hat never comes off. I get it, you don't want to ruin the holiday spirit, or maybe you are just planning to leave that to the HR Grinch to handle on Monday, but here's the skinny: that HR Grinch may pay you a visit as well if you didn't handle your own mess. So, if someone starts acting a little silly, pull them aside, nip that in the bud, and probably call an Uber.

Non-Managers: have fun, but remember that regardless of where it is held, it's still a work event. Enjoy the food, the drinks, and the general merriment, but if you want to get sloshed and act like a complete fool - save it for another party.

And to my HR Peeps: remember, it could always be worse - Die Hard happened during an office Christmas party. "Yippie Ki-Yay, HR Manager!"

IT'S THE MOST WONDERFUL TIME OF THE YEAR FOR CONTRACTORS, TOO

In keeping with my holiday party theme from the last chapter, I figured I would throw another one out there that is often not fully understood - contractors and company events. Picture this with me: you and everyone else at ACME Widgets is talking about the upcoming Christmas party, and how much fun it is going to be. You see Carl the Contractor sitting in his cubicle, punching away at a spreadsheet. You start to ask him if he is coming, then you remember the note at the bottom of the email from HR: "This company sponsored event is for regular, full-time employees of the company. Contractors are not eligible to attend." So, you slink slowly away and try not to make eye contact.

This situation can be especially difficult with contractors that you develop close ties with; those whom you feel are just as much your co-worker as, well your co-workers. In fact, you may like them more than your co-workers, but the fact is, they are not co-workers, and therein lies the rub.

So, let's go back to Carl the Contractor. He's a good guy, does his work, is accurate, comes in on time and never overcooks his fish in the microwave (unlike Patrick in Purchasing). You like him, and don't think of him any differently than any of your co-workers. Then one day Carl gets it in his head that he is being done wrong in one way or another, and decides to call up Larry the Lawyer. Since he is a contractor, the company doesn't have much to worry about, at least not in this particular situation, because whatever burr he has under his saddle is employment related, so he can take it up with his employer, which is the staffing agency. Except that there is a concept called dual employment, which is where Carl says: "sure, I am paid by ABC Staffing, but my <u>real</u> employer is ACME Widgets." When asked what proof he has, one example he gives is that he goes to all company sponsored events, and employees go to company sponsored events. The plumber they contracted out to fix the leaky sink didn't get to come because he was a contractor. Carl may be <u>called</u> a contractor, but that's just logistics of how he is paid. He is really no different from anyone else in the organization. Of course, if that is his only example, I would venture to guess that he is probably not going to have much of a leg to stand on. Still, it can, at the minimum be a foothold which can be added to a small, but growing, list of things that can add to the perception that he is, in fact, an employee of the company (like how long he has worked for you, and the level of freedom he had to do his work).

The takeaway here is that you need to establish clear guidelines separating employees from contractors, which would include company-sponsored extracurricular events. These are things that are done for the benefit of the company's **employees**. By inviting contractors, you are blurring that line, which can ultimately lead to trouble.

Does this mean that you have to exclude them from everything? Not necessarily. The thing to look for is whether the company is providing some type of assistance to the event. Be it catering, prizes, or paying the contractor to attend the event, I would think long and hard on those situations. Going out as a group after work? I don't see an issue there as long as no one puts it on their corporate credit card or expenses it in any other way. Of course, as with anything I say, it is best to talk with your own HR peeps. Most of the time they don't bite.

Most of the time.

CLASS OF... WHAT'S IT TO YA?!?

I am confident in my assessment that you are smart. If you weren't, you wouldn't be reading this book. In fact, I think this book is a gauge of above average intelligence, and may very well be used to determine IQ in the not so distant future. So, since you are smarter than the average schmo, you probably are aware that you cannot ask someone their age during a job interview. It's bad juju as well as generally being against the law. Yet seemingly intelligent people, some of whom may be holding this book, still ask job applicants their age.

They just may not realize it.

"I see you graduated from Permian High School, what year did you graduate?" is an example. You don't have to be a math whiz to know that since I graduated high school in 2016 that I am probably around 21 years old, give or take.

The bottom line is this: why do you need to know when I graduated from high school? What is your business reason for knowing that? Sure, it may be a requirement that they have a high school diploma or equivalent, but simply asking "do you have a high school diploma or equivalent?" gets the job done and keeps you out of hot water.

There are other variations of this as well that I have encountered in the few years since I graduated from high school. "In looking at your resume, I see you graduated from college here, how many years did it take you to finish?" This is usually followed by

"Were you a traditional student?" Alright, I can give you the first one - if someone took 10 years to get an undergraduate degree, you might want to know a little bit more - like did they change majors, or work two full-time jobs, or did they just really, really, really like college life (and therefore may have trouble adjusting to the real world...) But why does it matter if they were a traditional student, meaning they went straight from high school to college? Coupling those two questions together, you can very easily get within a couple of years of someone's age.

Do you think I am making a big deal out of this? Maybe, but let's think about this for a minute: why would I think that someone who thinks they are qualified for a job, who doesn't get said job, and may be strapped for cash - which would explain why they are looking for a job in the first place - try and sue you? You don't need a high school diploma to figure that one out.

SECTION 3

Putting the Human back in Human Resources

HITS, MISSES, AND TARGETS

Note: What follows is a blog I wrote just following a new year. While this is an example, it is an exercise I have found to be very effective where I look back and think on what has worked, what hasn't, and what I plan to do going forward. While this is a public sample, I have made a habit of doing this almost daily. Essentially ending my day with a quick rundown of the day, and a listing of what went well for me (to reinforce), what I wish I had done better (to avoid repeats), and my targets for the next day, week, month, etc. (to keep higher-level goals on the horizon).

Before this new year gets too far along, I want to look back on last year and review the hits (those things I am proud of), the misses (those things I am not so proud of), and my targets for the coming year (what I am looking forward to). I'm not one for resolutions, but that doesn't stop me from getting caught up in the moment of the New Year. Besides, if I am being completely honest, this happens to be my least favorite time of the year; I frequently refer to January as "the doldrums" because the weather is cold, the days are short, and unlike November and December, you don't have any holidays to look forward to. Add to this the fact that being the first of the year, people are back from their holiday vacations and are hammering out performance reviews and dealing with all those "little things" (which is manager speak for personnel issues) that they didn't want to deal with during the month of December, and my head just starts to hurt.

Hits

Let me start by taking a few moments and reflect on those things that went well this past year:

First off, I genuinely made good use of my available time-off. That's not to say I went to Hawaii or backpacked through the Peruvian Rainforest, nor were the number of days I took off particularly substantial. What I mean is, I <u>allowed</u> myself to be off, so that when I came back I was genuinely renewed. While I didn't completely turn my phone off, I did turn off all work-related notifications and gave myself permission to not check in. The crazy part? The place was still standing when I got back.

I didn't just enjoy my time off, though. I made better use of my time. About half-way through the year, I revisited David Allen's *Getting Things Done*, which I have probably read at least three times before, and just as before I gleaned some new nuggets and gained some additional inspiration. One thing this read through did was prompt a brain dump – that is to <u>get everything out of my head</u> and into a "system" and then keep my mind clear by moving new stuff into this system as soon as it pops into my mind, thus freeing up my mind for other things. This is not to say that I achieved mastery; there have definitely been times when I fell face first off the wagon, but I definitely saw an improvement on what I was able to accomplish and the peace of mind that comes from not having all that stuff sloshing around in my noggin.

Next up, as part of my time management revival, I made a <u>recurring reminder to read one professional article or blog every day</u> – not just business days, but *every* day. Did I knock this out every day? I wish I could say yes, but it definitely made me more cognizant of keeping up with things in my industry and profession.

While we are on the topic of recurring time management activities, I realized that if this was going to be my system, it had to be <u>my</u> system; I can't create separate islands for my personal and my professional life as I have tried (unsuccessfully) to do for so long. To that end, I also realized that if I was to include what is truly important on the list, then my to-do list needed to include what was truly important to me – quiet time, prayer, reminders to check on my wife if she wasn't feeling well, to-dos to text Mom and entries to plan camping trips with my son. Remembering to get my expense reports in are important, but what about my spiritual life, my family, and my friends? It is my system after all.

Misses

If I glossed over this section I would be doing myself a major disservice. In fact, this is probably the most important piece in the whole exercise. To ignore those things that didn't quite go right is to miss opportunities to correct and improve.

To that end, the main miss for me is worrying too much about what other people think. It seems like a small thing, but it is a key domino in that when it falls it knocks a lot of others down with it. Too often I find myself so caught up in worrying what other people might think that I am too hesitant to speak up and present ideas that might be seen as radical, or because other people might talk about me behind my back. In short, too often pride has gotten in the way of my best work. This has spilled into my personal life as well, and was made evident to me on a camping trip I took with my son to Garner State Park a few summers back.

For the uninitiated, Garner is perhaps the most popular state park in the great state of Texas, which is saying something. In addition to tubing the Frio River, one of its big draws is the dances held every night during the summer. I took my son to the dance, not because I thought he would want to dance, but rather because I thought he would enjoy watching everyone else. I was wrong. This time he decided to join in on the action and dance, and he danced the only way he knew how, which is a far sight from the line dancing and two-stepping that is the norm. Before I go any further, there are a couple of things you should know about Jordan: first, at the time of the dance, he was 13 years old and stood right at 6 feet. Second, he has Autism. Given his size and dance moves, he drew plenty of stares and turned a lot of heads. Sensing this, I stepped out and guided him back to our stone bench under a towering mesquite tree, where we sat for a few minutes before he told me he was ready to go back to camp. I told myself that I was protecting him from embarrassment, but the truth is I was protecting *myself*. The nice thing about Autism (at least in Jordan's case) is that he doesn't really concern himself with what other people think. He was having a great time and not hurting anyone, yet I stopped him because of my own fear of what others might think. I realized very soon what I had done and what my true motivation had been. Once again, my one and only son, the one with the "disability" had taught me a valuable lesson: How often have I stopped myself from asking questions, or speaking up because I was afraid of what others might think? How often had I not followed my instincts out of fear that I might be wrong? I should worry more about producing the best work possible and less time being concerned with what others might think. I should worry more about pursuing excellence and less about negative feedback along the way. I should just dance.

Targets

So, I have talked about when I have hit the mark, as well as when I've missed the mark, now let's talk about some of the targets I am going to aim for this year.

First: I am going to write more. A lot more. Not just blog, but other projects as well; fiction, non-fiction, sci-fi, cookbooks, romance, buddy comedies, screenplays, essays – whatever makes me happy. I have always enjoyed the act of writing, or rather the act of creating, but when I go back and look at what I have come up with I am never happy. I know I am not going to be up for a Pulitzer Prize any time soon, but I also know that I am my harshest critic. Just like the dance at Garner, I am afraid to get out there because I am afraid of what others will say.

Second, I am going to nurture my professional network. In years past I have focused on expanding it, and while I don't regret that, it is time to nurture and grow what I have. Like a farmer acquiring land from his neighbors, if he continues to only buy and doesn't work what he has, he is missing out on the benefits his existing land can yield.

This list isn't intended to be all-inclusive; for one thing, it will definitely grow as the year progresses and I am sure that I will look back around this time next year and gush (or lament) over something that I am proud (or ashamed) of that didn't make the list. The main thing is that I expand upon the good stuff and learn from the rest.

COMPETITION

I've got a question for you: Who is your competition?

I mean YOUR competition, not your company's. Who stands in the way of YOU getting YOUR best work done? Who stands in the way of YOU achieving YOUR goals?

If you work in a support function, like HR, it is often your very own internal customers.

Let's start by talking about competition, namely what it really is. In its purest sense competition is just someone, or something, <u>competing</u> for your business. If you own a McDonald's and there is a Burger King right next to you, that Burger King is your competition. Maybe your customers prefer McDonald's to Burger King, but if your customer service leaves something to be desired, they very well may decide they like Burger King better.

How is this different from whatever services you offer your (internal) customers? What happens if your customer decides that it is easier to go it alone rather than call you because you are a pain in the rump to deal with. Even though you are the undisputed subject matter expert, you are now competing with your customer...

So, what do you do?

The same thing you would do if you were running any other kind of business - you make it so that working with you is the best option available. You make the competition unfavorable when compared to what you offer, and not just because you are the expert and have years of training and experience. You make it easier for your customer to work with you than for them to go at it alone.

I am telling you this because as HR people, we tend to feel that if our customers don't follow our advice, something really bad is going to happen. We are convinced that they will get sued, lose, get fired - and then they will be sorry; they will wish they had listened to us then! You laugh (or maybe not, I may be the only one who thought that was funny), but it is not that far off the mark. But what happens when they don't lose? They become emboldened. "Look what I did," they say. I avoided all the crap that goes with dealing with that nutty HR guy and nothing happened." Then they do it again (by "it" I am referring to not partnering with you), and if nothing happens, they do it again, and so on, and you lose professional credibility each and every time. Sure, it may eventually catch up to them, but by then it is too late and nobody wins. This goes not just for HR, but anyone who provides a service to the business. Maybe the outcome isn't getting sued, but everyone has some kind of worst-case scenario, but what happens when the worst-case doesn't happen, or at least not right away?

IT REALLY IS WHO YOU KNOW

You seem like a person of above average intelligence, so I am going to let you in on a little piece of free advice.

Get to know the boss' Administrative Assistant

By "get to know" them, I mean REALLY get to know them and (this is critical here) treat them as well as, if not better than, you treat the boss. I am not kidding here - they can literally make or break your relationship with the boss.

I once worked for a woman who was very hard to read. Actually, that is putting it mildly. She was <u>impossible</u> to read, and I make a living reading people. This was problematic for me because I would often have to go to her with news that was not always great, and when it comes to news, just like anything else, delivery is important. If someone is having a particularly rough day you may need to add a little sugar to help the medicine go down. With this particular boss, it was hard to know when, or how much, sugar needed to be applied.

Enter her amazing Administrative Assistant. Early in my tenure, I sat down with her and asked point blank: "how do you know if she is having a bad day?" The Admin smiled and said: "her hair. It'll be flat." Unfortunately, I didn't have time to get more specifics so I thanked her, started observing, and sure enough - if it was a flat hair day, I did well to alter my approach. Why her hair was flat is beyond me, but honestly it isn't relevant. What <u>is</u> relevant is that by simply talking with the Administrative Assistant, my job got a whole lot easier.

Another example involves a company where I did a little consulting work, then joined full time. In this particular instance, the President was, well, volatile. One minute I could get anything I needed, the next I was challenged over the most minute detail. So, I approached his longtime Administrative Assistant and asked for advice. She advised me to never schedule a meeting with him in the morning. She went on to tell me that his morning routine was to first review all his production reports from the day before and make sense of them, and any interruptions were never welcomed. Next he liked to talk with his production leaders to talk about the previous day and see how things were looking for the present day. By the time he wrapped that up, he would start getting hungry, rapidly moving to "hangry," and would stay like that until he ate. She told me that she actually liked to take lunch early because he was too difficult to deal with in the hour before he would go to eat. I took her advice and anytime I needed something from him I went to see him in the afternoons and found a much more receptive, and less hangry, ear.

So, while everyone else tries to get to know our bosses, their habits, their ticks, and what they like and what they don't like; you can use the often-overlooked shortcut - the person who knows the boss better than anyone else.

HR BULLIES

Every profession has people who get into it for the wrong reasons. While these people are usually in the minority, they are often the ones who create negative stereotypes for everyone else.

HR is no exception.

For us, these people are often the ones who go into HR thinking that they will have some type of control or authority over others, and are the ones who will tell you "no" simply because they can. They will look at you and say "I'm sorry, but you can't promote this person because the job description says you have to have 5 years experience, and they have 4 and a half." They are the people who will throw around fancy legal terms and academic theories and expect you to fall in line because it all sounds fine and good.

They are HR Bullies, and just like the kids on the playground (or now online), they are the ones who feel inferior in some capacity, so they overcompensate in another. For those of us who have to deal with the carnage these people create for our profession, I have a request:

Fight them!

Push back!

Make them explain what the legal term that they just threw out means.

Ask them to educate you on the "halos and horns" effect (or whatever they are spouting off).

Explain to them that you understand there are going to be risks, but you want to better understand those risks so you can make an informed business decision. Remind them that at the end of the day it is your call (you, the manager). You are the one who will have to answer for it if the decision goes south and if they can't get their heads around the concept take it up the chain until you get someone who does get it.

Just like a schoolyard bully, if you push back these people will either adapt or go somewhere else. If they adapt, score one for the good guys. If they go somewhere else, they may still sully my beloved profession, but at least you won't have to deal with them.

THE PROBLEM WITH TITLES: YOU CAN'T EAT 'EM

One thing that never ceases to amaze me is the importance people put on titles.

I am reminded of an old skit from Cheers (Millennials, ask your parents) where Rebecca convinces Woody, who has just approached her for a raise, that he doesn't want a raise, he wants a title. Of course, hilarity ensues. While this episode is about 30 years old (yikes!) it takes a jab at something that I still see today, which is the weight people put on titles.

So, how important is a title to you? Would you change jobs over one? Would you hold out for a title and pass on an otherwise great opportunity? If you said "nevah! Not me!" my question to you is this: is that the <u>logical</u> you talking? Have you actually been in that situation? I ask because you would be surprised at how many people fall into the same trap as Woody (hint: in that episode, "Our Hourly Bread," Sam and Carla also fall for it.)

So, why do seemingly rational people (and sitcom actors) put unnecessary weight on titles and pass up on other, more tangible things? Because it relays a sense of who we are. It gives us a sense of accomplishment. At one point in time, I was the HR Director for a small manufacturing company that had an HR department of one. If you aren't that good at math, this simply means that I had one direct report which was the man in the mirror. In other words,

I did everything. I enjoyed my time there, but after a while I decided it was time to pursue other opportunities. I remember talking to one hiring executive in particular who told me outright that his only concern was my title, since this position was a Sr. Manager role. Never mind that the company was 10 times the size and the pay was better, it wasn't a Director slot. I told him that it was about the work, about the opportunity, about the "tangibles" and that the title wasn't relevant to me, but he simply couldn't get past it.

Look, I get it. In terms of career progression, you don't want to appear that you are going backward, but which position has more clout: Director of Widgets at Willie's One-man Widget factory or Manager of Widget Manufacturing, North America for William, Wayne, and Watson Widgets Worldwide? Which one is going to look better on a resume, and more importantly, which is going to grow you professionally?

CULTURE CLUB

Recently I was reading an interesting, and telling, Glassdoor post by someone who had interviewed at a particular company. The post ended with the writer concluding that all of the positive reviews for this company were fake, citing the frequent use of the word "culture." He/she stated, and I quote: "No one but HR writes 'great culture' NO one."

Ouch.

But is there some truth to that? I mean I tout my organization's culture all the time, but... I work in HR.

I don't think anyone would disagree that an organization's culture isn't a key to whether you want to come to work there, but are we articulating it well? Not only that, but do we really know what our organization's culture even is? If you were to climb into an elevator going up 10 floors with a job applicant, would you be able to describe your organization's culture in a way that the candidate could actually understand? Really understand - not "we have a culture of accountability," or "our culture treats everyone like family."

How about, "people take pride in their work here, so if you see this as a 'job,' you aren't going to like it here." Or, as was described to me about another company I worked for: "we bleed (company color) here." On the flip side, if you are honest, does your elevator speech sound something like: "we don't care about what we do, we just care about what our boss sees us doing." Or, "so long as you don't make any mistakes or ask too many questions, you will be fine." If your truthful response is on the less positive side of the equation, what are you doing about it? If the answer is "nothing," ask yourself if you aren't part of the problem. Don't worry, you won't need to take an elevator ride to come to the answer. You'll know before you push the button.

KENNY ROGERS: HR PRO EXTRAORDINAIRE

"You gotta know when to hold 'em. Know when to fold 'em. Know when to walk away, and know when to run."
- The Gambler, Kenny Rogers

No book on HR would be complete without at least touching on the timeless wisdom of Kenny Rogers. When I look at his catalogue of music, I am all but convinced that he was in HR before pursuing the less noble path of super-stardom. To name a few HR-related hits:

"Lucille" (Turnover)
"Daytime Friends" (Office Romance)
"She Believes in Me" (Performance Reviews)

But today I want to focus on arguably Kenny's biggest hit: "The Gambler," which deals us some critical career advice (see what I did there?)

You see, I have seen many a bright, hardworking and talented individual get sucked into a job they didn't like because they didn't know anything else. It is a classic case of Sunk Cost, which is the situation where we feel like we have invested so much time, money, energy, whatever, into something and therefore we push ahead. It doesn't matter that it doesn't light our fire. It doesn't matter that we don't enjoy doing it anymore, or that we even hate coming to work. The only thing that matters is that this is all we have done for so long, we have invested this part of our lives up to now doing this, it would feel like all that time has been wasted. The idea of doing something else - something that we may WANT to do, is not viable; not because we can't do it, but because it would mean that we have to turn away from all the time that we have put into learning our existing craft or trade. In other words, we have to "know when to hold 'em. Know when to fold 'em. Know when to walk away... and know when to run."

I love what I do, but I didn't always. I began my career as a Store Manager for an auto parts retailer. It wasn't a bad gig - I was paid fairly, I worked with some great people, and there were some good options for upward mobility (perhaps not with that particular company - they went out of business; but I could have easily been recruited away). The problem was, I didn't like it. So, I changed careers. Not once, but twice, and if I do get to a point where I have had my fill of HR, I am confident I will be able to walk away from the 25 years I have invested in it and do something that does light my fire. I'm not saying it will be easy, but I don't want to be known as "The Coward of the County" when it comes to my career.

MOTIVATION: THE GOOD, THE BAD, AND THE UGLY

In my line of work, I have seen a lot of ways managers have motivated their teams. You've heard of motivation, right? It is the subtle art of getting people to do what you want them to do. In my own unscientific way, I have concluded that motivation falls within one of three camps: The (Really) Good, the (Not Too) Bad and the (Down Right) Ugly.

Let's start with the Ugly. This is where the manager coerces his or her subordinates to do his or her bidding. The employee performs the task so that they do not face the wrath of their manager or supervisor. Have you ever worked for someone like that? I know I have. This is the kind of boss whose staff doesn't take vacation at the same time as the boss because these are the good days at the office. In situations like this, there is no upside to doing a good job. Employees are paid to do a job, so that is what they do. If they screw up, they go into CYA mode, which usually consists of finger pointing and coverups. The result of this management approach is that your good employees are going to leave at the first opportunity while your poor performers stick around until some other sucker is fool enough to hire them or you fire them and start the dance all over again. Your reputation starts to leak out on places like Glassdoor, social media, and career sites, then good help becomes even more elusive.

Next up we have the (Not Too) Bad, which is the classic carrot and stick mentality. You establish clear rewards for desired actions and consequences for undesired behaviors. Do this thing that you are supposed to do - and you get rewarded. Do this thing that you are not supposed to do, and you get punished, or at least miss out on a reward. This can work on an individual level, or for a group. I have never worked in fast food, but I know someone who did. She referred to receiving a "Fry Bonus," which in my understanding was a quality control mechanism to incentivize employees not to be too liberal (or conservative) with the fries. The store brought in a set number of fries and, through careful calculation, knew how many various combinations of small, medium and large fries this should amount too. If the store came within a certain range of this target, everyone got a small bonus on their checks. Too many fries in the bottom of the bag? No Fry Bonus. Not enough fries in the cardboard holder, and thus making the customer consider patronizing another drive-thru window? No Fry Bonus. I'm not knocking it, my friend certainly appreciated the gesture, and I'm sure it helped ensure the efficient distribution of those little slivers of salty, deep-fried potato heaven, but it just seems like a lot of work to get a desired result.

Finally, we have the (Really) Good. This is the point where employees are beyond motivated - they are inspired. Their sense of pride in the organization trumps coercion and even motivators. People who are in this state work in the best interest of the organization. Period. When something needs to get done, they roll up their sleeves and get it done, without either expectation of reward or fear of punishment. The funny thing about this level is that I am not sure how to get there. I did some work for a company where the majority of the people were truly inspired. They pulled together as a team and the sense of pride in this place was absolutely palatable, in-spite of the fact that:

- The pay was directly in line with the market
- The benefits were below average at best

- PTO was slightly above non-existent
- Being driven by two people who, by their own admission, could not work anywhere else because no one would hire them (their words, not mine).

Yet the company saw year over year top-line growth in the 20-30 percent range, even during the Great Recession. I am still in touch with people who are there and the company continues to set new sales records which, if I am being completely honest is mind-boggling to me. How can a company with average pay, crappy benefits and an ego-centric, undereducated leadership team hire, retain, and motivate great talent? Well, duh! They hired me! OK, their success was well underway before I started. In fact, it was what drew me to the company in the first place. The only thing I can put my finger on is that everyone in the company felt that he or she had a hand in the company's success and therefore they took pride in the place where they worked. This was driven by the leadership which, despite all its faults, clearly had something going for it.

So, what are you doing to foster that sense of communal success? What are you doing to build pride in your organization? Are you holding your employee's jobs over their heads? Are you throwing money at them every time they start to grumble? Are you enticing them with better titles or closer parking spaces? Tossing them other perks like memberships to the fruit of the month club (the gift that keeps on giving the whole year)?

Do you lord your position over them and pull rank just because you can? Or are you inspiring ownership? Are you giving them something to truly be proud of? Are you showing integrity and honesty? Are you open and truthful in your communication?

SUMMER TIME, SWEET SUMMER TIME

When I'm not working, one of my favorite things to do is go camping. Lucky for me, my son loves it almost as much as I do. My wife is game as well, so long as at the bare minimum, there is air conditioning, but I can't fault her there - Texas can get brutal in the summer months. At any rate, my summers are usually filled with camping trips and other family adventures.

In fact, I am writing this while on one such adventure: my annual husband/wife trip to the Frio River. A tradition my wife and I have engaged in for twenty years now where we wrap up the summer with a final trip to the Texas Hill Country and float down the Frio River. Earlier today I was relaxing and catching up on some reading while my wife was taking a shower (another amenity she struggles to be without) when I came across an article that advocated giving up your to-do list, citing that it actually makes you less productive. I read the article with interest but finished it concluding that it was something I would have to disagree with. Like any good article though, it did get me thinking. The primary reason the article gave is research that has shown that keeping a tally of what you need to do (and therefore a list of what you haven't done, or need to get done), in fact brings you down - essentially eating at your mojo. This, in turn, makes you less productive because we all know that we are more productive when we are happy.

I can hear you asking now: "so what, exactly, does any of this have to do with you, Mr. Jim Perkins - HR geek, camping freak,

JIM PERKINS

Frio River lover, husband of an outdoorswoman who loves a hot shower and A/C as much as anyone, and your summer vacations?"

I'm glad you asked.

You see, I take these little trips - weekends here, 3–4 days there, and go somewhere that I enjoy and where I will have fun. I love camping because a.) I love being outside and b.) it gives me an unmatched chance to spend time with my son and if I am super lucky, my wife. As a bonus, my cellphone usually doesn't work, so I'm forced to unplug. Luckily I have always had bosses who respected that need for vacation (some more than others - you know who you are). At the end of the day, some would say that it was a win-win all the way around: I enjoy my time away from the office and the office enjoys some time without me.

I know, I know, I still haven't gotten to the point, so here goes: let go, baby. Just as they argued that having all that crap lingering on your lists can bring you down and thus mess with your productivity, so can not getting a change of scenery. You don't need 4 weeks of vacation to get a break. Plan a weekend getaway and either go somewhere that you can't get cell coverage or at the bare minimum, turn notifications off. Let folks know you will be out of pocket and delayed in responding. By delayed, I mean that you'll catch up to them when you're back in the office.

HELP WANTED

Over-education a must, lack of relevant experience a strong plus

When was the last time you looked for work, or just looked at job postings in general? How many called for, at the minimum, a bachelor's degree? Did you stop and look at the job itself and wonder whether the job was something that really called for a 4-year degree?

As an HR practitioner, I run across this from time to time (meaning a lot of times). Folks decide to post a job and, thinking about requirements, often the first thing that pops in their mind is college degree. As I have studied this, I have concluded that oftentimes this is not so much about the training or knowledge that the degree imparts, as it is about the biases the hiring manager has towards the person that he or she visualizes in his or her mind. For example, someone with a college degree is going to be more professional, right? Of course! I have *never* had someone who is degreed *ever* do anything stupid. Or, someone with a college degree is going to have more grit, because obtaining a degree is hard work, right? Sure. I've never run into a degreed slacker. On the flip side, do you think it is possible that you, as a hiring manager, could overlook a (very) qualified candidate simply because they don't have the degree? Put another way, how important is that piece of paper to you? Is it essential? A nice-to-have? Or maybe you just slapped it on there because you wanted to "upgrade the position."

"I hear ya Jim, and you know what? My HR Pain-in-the-Patooty already told me the same thing, so we made the degree preferred. We're good now." Sure, but how many people without a degree aren't going to give you the time of day? How many perfectly qualified, non-degreed candidates are going to look at that job posting, see college degree and stop there? Or maybe they do see that it is preferred, but they figure they will be in the minority of applicants so decide to just move on? I say this because I (wait for it) talk to people, it is an occupational hazard.

Now there are some jobs where, due to licensing or the nature of the work, a degree would either be a necessity or at least a good indicator of success. Medical Doctors, for instance, have to be licensed. I, for one, do not want to go to someone who tells me that they did not go to medical school, but has lots of "on the job training." If that were to happen, I can pretty much guarantee that I will pull myself right up off that paper covered bench thing and hoof it right on out the door, possibly with my pants tucked under my arm.

So, what I am I suggesting?

Consider very hard how important the degree really is to you and the success of the position. Are you hiring a highly specialized position? Or maybe one which requires extensive licensing? In these cases, you may need a degree, or at least truly prefer it. If you are hiring an HR writer, on the other hand, any schmuck with a cardboard sign will do.

HIRING TIP FOR THE DAY: DON'T HIRE MINI-ME'S

Some of the best interviewing advice I ever received was pretty simple: don't hire people who are like you. It was given to me by a boss as we were talking about a candidate that I was considering hiring for my team.

"Jim," he said, "this is a good candidate, but not for you. He is too much like you." This burned me up until I hired someone who was not like me, someone who turned out to be awesome.

I have sat in on several interviews where I felt like I was talking to a clone of the person doing the hiring. In those situations, I can't help but wonder: is the manager high on this person because they are the most qualified, or because they are someone that they wouldn't mind going to lunch with?

When you are looking to fill positions in your team, be sure and look at the whole picture and everything the candidates you like bring to the table. We all have gaps in our knowledge, skills, and abilities, so doesn't it make sense that when you are looking to hire someone, you would look for people who will fill as many of those gaps as you possible? Not only will this person help you, but you will help them as well.

Now back to fit. I think that fit is important - if you hire someone you can't stand simply because they are the polar opposite of you,

you are setting yourself up for trouble. They need to fit the team and be someone that you can work with. If the only person who fits that description is someone whose personality mirrors yours, I think you may have a problem, though.

So, what is the secret sauce?

Ask others for help, namely people who do not do the same thing as you do. Ask HR (not just the Recruiter) to interview them, and then be <u>open</u> and <u>receptive</u> to the feedback. Tell them that you are looking for someone to compliment you and your team, and while you like this particular candidate, you also want to be sure that they will make the team stronger. Sometimes an extra set of eyes is all you really need.

GOOD HELP IS HARD TO FIND

So are Good Drug Mules

I just returned from doing my civic duty, more commonly known as jury duty, where I was selected along with 11 other people to try a drug case. The defendant was a drug trafficker charged with possession with the intent to distribute around 7 Kilograms of cocaine. I won't bore you with the details, other than that the case revolved around the question of whether the guy on trial had actual "control" of the product, as opposed to just being along for the ride. Long story short, we convicted him - in all of 10 minutes, based on the testimony of the two clowns who were actually observed in physical possession of the drugs.

While I hate to admit it, I found the whole thing fascinating and this gave me a glimpse into a different world that at the end of the day was a business, though with some very keen differences, especially as it relates to HR. For example, in every company I have worked, employee discipline usually meant either a note to your file, a firm reprimand, maybe a suspension. I have yet to work for a company where employee discipline involved broken bones, missing fingers or toes or a shallow grave. In most mainstream organizations a major screw up might result in you getting fired, but nowhere has it involved a chainsaw. In addition, many companies have to keep up with government regulations, and failing to do so may result in fines. This is different from the risk of getting busted and sent up the river; suffering through prison food and a hairy cellie named Bart.

But for me, the most fascinating thing was the working conditions. I have seen a wide variety of working conditions and environments, but nothing like what I heard about in this trial. I listened as witnesses went into great detail regarding a typical day of pawning off this dude's dope, which often meant sitting outside a crack house until the buyer had cooked and sold enough to pay off what was owed him for the product. I'm talking <u>days</u> sitting in your car or outside on the lawn, unable to go anywhere, eating whatever the benevolent purveyor of this particular drug den decided to bring out to you.

As I'm hearing all this my HR mind started turning - how do you recruit for this line of work? What incentives do you offer? It's not like you get health insurance or a generous PTO package, so it must be the money. Drug dealers make a lot of money, right? While this is the case for some, as with any other job, there is a hierarchy. The big boss, whether it is the CEO or El Chapo, usually makes a nice living, but as you work your way down the line the pay goes down as well. At some point there are the entry-level positions, which in the case of this particular drug operation the pay ranges from between $500 and $1,000 for a trip; an amount, I might add, which was not pre-negotiated - they were literally at the mercy of the defendant and his generosity. They would deliver the drugs, sit in the car until the street dealer walked out with the cash, drive back, hand the cash to the benevolent drug dealer, who would peel off a few bills and hand it to them and send them on their way. Considering that the best-case scenario they would make a trip a week - which was simply how long it took to deliver the drugs and collect the money, I figured that at most they could look for was $52,000 a year - literally no time off. But the reality is they were making runs once, or in some cases twice, a month. That's $24,000 a year on the **high-end**. Sure, it is more than they might make working part-time at McDonald's, but there is something to be said for not being beheaded and hung from an overpass if you give someone a small order of fries when they, in fact, ordered a large.

So, we've established that the working conditions were lousy, the pay not really all that great - especially considering the risk involved, and the complete lack of benefits; this leaves me to wonder, how did he recruit? It's not like he could post on Indeed, or LinkedIn. The answer was deceptively simple: he networked. He worked with other people who were in the trade, who knew someone, who then knew someone else. Usually the someones that they knew had no prospects, either because they were too lazy to work, (as was the case of one of the witnesses we heard from) or they were virtually unemployable (like the other witness, who at the age of 23, had already served a 4-year sentence for burglary). The defense attorney, when he was cross-examining the second witness asked him why he would risk his life and freedom for one thousand dollars, and this streetwise thug teared up and said that he had never seen a thousand dollars at any one time. So yes, the money was crap, but it was still more crap than he had seen, and the defendant knew it. So, at the end of the day, money was his one and only carrot. The guy on trial didn't offer anything else to inspire loyalty. These guys knew that if they were caught, the gig was up. They also knew that he was intentionally separating himself from the dope so that if they were busted he could rack it up as a loss and they would do the time. Of course, it didn't work out that way.

How could he have done this differently? While I'm honestly not 100% sure, I do think that the heavy reliance on money, and money alone, might not be the best people strategy. So, Mr. Drug Dealer, if you are reading this from your prison cell, when you get out - in 15 years if you get parole - I hope you take this to heart. You were smart in how you handled the logistics of your deals. You were also smart in how you developed your network, but you failed miserably in how you managed your greatest asset: your people. Perhaps money is **your** greatest motivator, but that isn't so for everyone. Maybe next time you should do more for your employees, say a plaque after reaching a milestone like moving 10 Kilos without incident. Perhaps greater training in the event they are caught might be helpful (hint: when asked if there are drugs in the car, they shouldn't automatically say "yes," - that one's on me, free of charge). I say all of this, though I'm fairly certain that my chances of ever working as an HR Consultant for a part of a drug cartel were pretty much blown with this trial (no pun intended).

But there are a couple of lessons that those of us not employed in the illegal drug trade could learn from this experience as well. First, money is relative. As was proven to me, you can get people to take on a tremendous amount of risk for a relatively small amount of money, it is all dependent on their circumstances. However, and this leads me to my second point, if the only thing you have to motivate your employees is money, your employees will see their work as just a job and therefore will not be loyal towards you. If that is the case with you, don't be surprised when they jump ship for a better opportunity, even if that opportunity is 10 versus 15 years.

OK, maybe there is a third: crime doesn't pay. Especially if you take me out of work for a week to sit on your jury.

ADVICE TO JOB SEEKERS: ASK FOR THE SALE

Before I got into HR, I tried my hand at sales. It was a fun gig with a lot of autonomy, ability to set my hours, and since I often just needed a computer and phone it afforded me a lot of flexibility in where I could work. The only drawback was that the position was 100% commission, which is a nice way of saying no sales, no money. This small detail had a substantial impact on the length of my sales career, meaning I lasted less than a year.

Short stint aside, I learned a lot as I slid down this rabbit hole, with one of the most important things being to always ask for the sale. Asking for the sale is a different take on what we see in the movies where the Wall Street types are dialing and the manager comes out of his glass office only to impress upon those who aspire to be in the glass office to "always be closing." I suppose since I was in the south, management felt it was more polite to "ask" for something. "Always be closing" just sounds so pushy - too *New York* - and that will just never do.

The reason asking for the sale was seen as so critical to any salesperson's success was probably because most of us sucked at it - double that if you were new to the game. We would go in, make our pitch, get the prospective client primed and ready to buy, and then give them our business card and wait for their call.

This principle of asking for the sale applies to job seekers as well.

If you interview for a job, you are selling you. You are hawking your unique skills, abilities and, I hate to break this to you, personality. You are explaining to a prospective employer why they need look no further than you. Why they don't need to look at another resume because you are it: you are the bomb-dot-com and they need to hire you. In other words, you need to close the deal; you need to ask for the sale.

Closing the deal in an interview can take many different forms. There is the classic "so, when can I start?" approach, but that's just a little too cliché, and rarely comes across as authentic. There is the "this sounds very interesting, I would like to learn more," which for me is the interview equivalent of leaving your business card. You are so close, then you walk away and wait for them to call. If you are going to ask for the sale, you have to tell them that you are excited by what you have seen and/or heard, that it sounds like the perfect opportunity and you, in no uncertain terms, want to take the next step. I have seen many hiring manager's opinion shift when a candidate ended an interview by saying "this sounds like a great opportunity, I would love to be a part of this company/organization/team." Yet HARDLY ANYONE ACTUALLY SAYS THAT. In fact, I hear far more "so, when do I start?" than "this sounds like the perfect opportunity for me..." spiels.

How important do I think this is? Well, I honestly believe had I not done this myself, I may not have ever gotten into HR in the first place and you would not be reading this book, and you would go through life unfulfilled. When I interviewed for my first job in HR I ended the interview knowing that it was what I wanted to do, I was stoked! So, at the end of the interview, I looked the nice lady square in the eye and said: "I am very excited about this opportunity, and would love to come to work here." Not long after that first interview that nice lady went on to become one of my favorite bosses and a great mentor to me.

Need more proof?

About a year after beginning to work for said nice lady we were having lunch and I brought up my interview. She told me that I was the only person she interviewed who actually said that they wanted the job. Now I know that isn't the only reason I got the job; my timeless good looks and unmatched charm did most of the work - but telling her that I wanted it obviously didn't hurt.

SOMETIMES IT'S BEST TO DANCE WITH WHO YOU BROUGHT

Not everyone is as likable as me. I'll admit it, I'm humble that way. So, just like me, you've no doubt found yourself in situations where you have had to work with people who were less than pleasant, or worse, maybe you <u>hired</u> them and they misrepresented their skills to you in the selection process. To make matters worse, these things are coming to a head now that things are really getting rolling, which isn't all that surprising because people's true colors or skills often don't show until the heat is on.

So, what do you do?

Move them off the project?

Fire them?

Take them out back and use them as a speed bump?

This is up to you, but before you make any rash decisions I just ask that you think it all the way through, because sometimes it's best to dance with who you brought. Sure, there may be a pretty young thing standing all by herself next to the punch bowl looking absolutely stunning in her pink chiffon dress and shoes that are dyed to match, but does it really make sense to approach her when the next REO Speedwagon song comes on? Sure, maybe you "can't fight this feeling anymore," but what are you going to do when the lights come up and you have "to bring this ship into the shore?" Are you ready to "throw away the oars...forever?"

It may seem obvious: "yeah, yeah, I can't go off half-cocked, I get it," but the fact is managers who go off half-cocked have kept many an HR Pro in work. I have often heard things like "they are poisoning the team," or "it only takes one bad apple," and while I agree with these sentiments, let's face it: sometimes we (and by we, I'm including myself) exaggerate. If we exaggerate someone's damage to a project or team, sometimes you end up cutting someone loose only to find that, while they weren't doing a great job, they were still doing a job. If you remove them now, you lose whatever benefit - regardless of how small - they bring right now.

So, do you stick out and just hope they quit? That is not what I am recommending. Put on your manager britches and counsel them. Have the tough conversations about what you expect and what you are getting. Let them get defensive if they are going to, and/or accept their apologies if they apologize. Be consistent, and if the gap remains, consider your options. Of course, it would probably make sense to start thinking about the next dance and who you are going to ask. In other words, start recruiting.

WHAT GETS MEASURED GETS, WELL... MEASURED

Like most HR people I love me some metrics, and not just in my professional life. I get stoked over metrics of all sorts, though admittedly I like some better than others. If the metric makes me feel good, like the miles-per-gallon on my wife's hybrid, I'm happy. If the metric is less favorable, like the MPG on my SUV, I don't tout that so much.

But back to HR... One area in our blessed field that we love to metric up is recruiting, and why not? It's easy! You can track things like the number of days the position has been open, number of applicants, and number of interviews; but the one that everyone really cares about is the time it takes to fill a position - aka Time to Fill. In fact, if John Grisham had started out in HR instead of being an attorney, I'm certain his first novel would have been called "a Time to Fill." In many organizations, it is the main yardstick by which recruiters are graded. If a position has a long T2F, the manager starts getting antsy, which makes the recruiter antsy. Sadly, often when the recruiter gets antsy the *quantity* of candidates goes up, and the *quality* of candidates goes down. Instead of sending along an average of 1 in 50 applicants, they start sending along 1 in 25. Instead of stepping back and looking at where we are sourcing, they double down because to stop and regroup would only add more days. The end result: the hiring manager ends up settling for a less than ideal candidate because they are sick of interviewing.

Now enter the HR metrics. When you think of a purely HR metric, what is the first thing that comes to mind? If you answered "turnover" you are probably in the majority. Just in case you are wondering, turnover is nothing more than a gauge of how many people, as a percentage of your workforce, are leaving your organization. If you lost 10 people last year, and your average headcount is 100, you have a 10 percent turnover rate. Higher turnover is generally seen as bad and as such, HR geeks tend to use it as a measure of a manager's effectiveness. High turnover is seen as a sign of poor morale, poor training, unfavorable work conditions, and... wait for it... poor hiring practices. If you are not hiring for fit, you are going to lose people, either voluntarily (they leave) or involuntarily (they get asked to leave). Now, I will be the first to say that sometimes turnover is necessary. Maybe you inherited a team that is making an Olympic sport of surfing the internet, and it is time to make some adjustments. Or maybe your organization is going through some lean times and so you are having to trim back. These aren't necessarily a sign of a bad manager (in the case of the former, I would argue the opposite to be true).

But here's the deal: when it comes to people, we all too often operate in silos. Managers say they want the best people, then berate the recruiting team for a time-to-fill ratio that is high. Managers and HR need to make recruiting *success* a top priority, so maybe instead of Time to Fill, we measure Quality of Applicant. For instance, on a scale of 1-10, 1 being "That was 30 minutes of my life I will never get back," to 10 being "<Profanity>! I need to hire them! Like yesterday!" Rate all the applicants that you (HR or Manager) interview and come up with an average score. The message you are sending to the recruiter is simple: you send me crap, you ain't gonna look so good. To be clear, for this to work it has to have a long tail. Even the best recruiter out there isn't a mind reader, so the first few interviews probably aren't going to hit the top mark, which is why I liken them to sharpening a knife

- the more interviews (or swipes down the stone), the better the candidates (sharper the knife). Of course, this only works if you are quick, open, and candid with feedback. If the recruiter is getting this feedback and being measured by the right things I will be willing to bet that they will start slicing through bad candidates like hot butter.

(DON'T) POUR SOME SUGAR ON ME

Now for a quick message to corporate recruiters and hiring managers: your company is not perfect. I don't care how many times you have made the #1 spot on whatever "Best Places to Work" list, or how low your turnover is, or how happy everyone seems - every organization has warts. Sure, some warts are bigger than others, and some of those warts have hair growing out of them, but regardless, everyone has them and we all know it. So why is it that when we are interviewing we tell people how great it is going to be if they join us, how well everyone gets along, how office politics don't apply to us, how much everyone loves to come to work every day, and how we wish we didn't have to go home at night...

What are we accomplishing when we do this? Are we increasing our odds of getting the right candidate or are we simply filling holes? Are we looking for the best fit, or are we managing to a number? We may get some great folks, but it is a gamble as to whether or not they are going to fit in with your organization.

What if we lay ourselves bare when we are talking to people. "Look, this is a great place to work, but like everywhere else, we have some warts. We have been losing market share, and as a result, we have had to shake things up. People are in different roles than they were before, and others have been exited from the company. This position is open because the person who was here before wasn't a good fit. Further, once we fill this role, we will likely restructure again and there are a few people who will either be in entirely different positions or will not be with the company.

What I am looking for is someone who is willing to come in and roll up their sleeves and help move us forward. We can, and will, turn things around and I hope you are the kind of person who can do that with us."

If you go with door number 2, you are going to have some people tell you something along the lines of either: they are going to stay where they are at or, thanks for taking the time to chat, but this is not the place for them. It is going to hurt sometimes because some of those folks will have interviewed well, and/or came highly recommended, and/or had a great resume, and/or etc. but they will likely have not been a good fit in the long run. Yes, you would have filled a void, ticked a box, reduced a number, but how long before the new wears off and you are looking at that same empty void, unticked box, or increased number?

CREAM ISN'T THE ONLY THING THAT RISES

We've all heard that the cream always rises. For me, this has often been used in reference to employees. Meaning that the best will rise to the top, stand out, and be noticed. As a good manager (and you know you are, you *are* reading this book, after all), you know that these are the employees you need to be developing and growing. These are the folks you want to be devoting your time to because they are going to give you the biggest return on your investment. They are the cream that you will skim off the top and make into nice, smooth pats of delicious butter.

But while you are skimming your cream you are also going to have other employees floating around taking up space as well: the turds. These are the ones who, like the cream, stand out, but not for the right reasons. When you come across the occasional floater bobbing around the key is to deal with it quickly and efficiently (with the help of your beloved HR person), and get back to tending to your cream. While this may seem obvious, all too often we think that we are spending our time developing our staff when in fact we are spending far too much time with those who aren't adding much, if any, value. Then you wonder why morale stinks <u>and</u> you don't have any butter for your rolls.

5 SECONDS

I recently received a text from a friend and former co-worker that said: "Do wonderful things today!" The person who sent this is someone who I have always had a great deal of respect for, personally and professionally, but I have to tell you though, this text put him on an even higher plane for me. And it took <u>maybe</u> 5 seconds to type.

As I thought on the text, I remembered a conversation I had with a different co-worker about her manager. I honestly can't remember what prompted the talk, only that the entire conversation centered around her manager, and how much she liked working for them, how the employee would do anything for them, etc, etc... It made my cold little HR heart go pitter-patter. After hearing example after example, I asked: "What is it that sets [the manager] apart as a great boss?" She sat there a minute, then said: "I don't know, I guess it is just the little things." When I asked what the little things were, she said that often times she would return to her desk from lunch, or a meeting, or even a restroom break and find a sticky note with a smiley face drawn on it and stuck to her computer. She knew that it was the manager who had left it, and it showed her the manager cared and appreciated her work. Again, a 5-second gesture that made a big difference. I am sure that there were other things that the manager did, but this drawing on a Post-it note was what stood out to me.

A whole industry has sprung up to help employers show appreciation to their employees. One estimate I saw was that companies spend between 1 and 2% of their payroll on incentive rewards, and I'm not sure if that includes team building exercises. Yet, according to Gallup, 51% of the U.S. workforce is not engaged.

I am not saying that random texts and sticky note smiley faces on computer monitors are going to cure this, because they ain't. In fact, in both of the above cases, the behavior was a manifestation from a manager who exhibited true caring and leadership.

So, if you are truly concerned about employee engagement, before you spend thousands of dollars and an entire day on a "team building" exercise, think about something a little more granular; something that would take, I don't know, 5 seconds. Then repeat.

SO, YOU SAY WANT A(N) (R)EVOLUTION

I have worked with a number of business leaders who have made attempts at instituting some form of change. As I am sure you can imagine, the success of these endeavors spreads across a continuum from a.) outright, flat on your face, failures, to z.) blazing successes. While there are a lot of facets that go into where on the spectrum any particular change will fall into, one factor that has often preceded the most successful campaigns has been where the leader proposes the change as an *evolution*, not a *revolution*.

When change is approached as an evolution, the leader recognizes that there will be challenges along the way and that perhaps not everything will work exactly as he or she anticipates. The leader essentially starts off the initiative with something along the lines of: "look, I have a vision, but I need your help with the execution." It is a humbling proposition to say that you don't know everything, but it can pay off in spades when the rubber meets the road. This is because instead of feeling as though a change is being shoved down their throats, the team feels that if something doesn't work the leader will work to correct it.

So, if you are implementing a major change consider whether it is more important to be a revolution (a quick change), or an evolution (maybe a little slower). I'm not saying revolutions aren't necessary – had one not happened, I might be typing this as a citizen of Mexico (I call Texas home, remember). Sometimes you simply need to rip the Band-Aid off and get it over with. There simply isn't isn't any time for discussion. In a lot of situations, if there is going to be pain it is best to get as much of that out of the way up front as possible so folks can begin healing. Once that is done, you shift your focus to making the group successful.

On the flip side, if we are talking about discomfort with the change, as opposed to outright pain, consider letting it evolve and allow for genuine buy-in. Hopefully, your team is *collectively* smarter than you. If not, that's another issue altogether.

WIKIWORK

I hired an executive once who cold called the company when he had received an offer to get the skinny on what it was like to work there. He told me that he called the receptionist and asked to speak to someone in a given department, and she connected him. He then told them that he was considering working for us, and wanted to know what they thought of the company. He said that he did this every time before changing companies, and while he said that occasionally the person on the other end would reply with a standard, "I'm really not comfortable talking about this," most of the time people would open up.

Changing jobs is a big move and, as he put it, what is the worst that the company could have done? Rescind the offer? If they had, it would have been a clear sign that he didn't want to work there anyway. Fast-forward to today and you have... Glassdoor, or as we in HR call it: "OhcrapsomeonepostedtoGlassdoor!"

You probably are familiar with Glassdoor, but for the benefit of my Mom, who occasionally reads my blog and might even read this book, Glassdoor is that lovely platform that allows you to anonymously rate - and by extension - review pretty much any company out there.

Now, as my comment earlier about HR's nickname for Glassdoor would imply, there are a lot of HR people out there who hate Glassdoor. They will tell you that happy employees don't take the time to go out and do a review. They say it is nothing more than a haven for disgruntled employees to complain. Tell that to the fine folks at Silverline CRM. They have a 4.9 out of 5 stars on Glassdoor. Perusing their comments for cons, I saw things like "working remotely means I don't get to hang out with all of these awesome people on a regular basis," and "we're growing fast, which comes with your typical growing pains. However, I feel like it's been handled well."

The point of all this is simple - the workforce is moving more and more to a pure market economy. Gone are the days of the great company myth with the manager telling everyone how great they have it because they work for a big company, or a well-respected market leader, or whatever.

If you work in customer service, I would venture to bet that you pay attention to your company's Yelp! reviews. If you are an HR Pro, do you pay attention to your Glassdoor reviews? How do they stack against your internal engagement surveys? If there is a discrepancy, that might be a whole other can of worms. My challenge - to myself as much as to my HR cronies - let's start paying attention to those reviews more. Maybe we can't all get 4.9s, but I would venture to guess we can all work to do better.

THE HR BLACK HOLE

Several years ago, I found myself looking to recruit a fellow HR Pro. After the usual round of online postings and social media, I went to a networking event geared towards HR folk, or at least people who purported to be HR folk.

The meeting consisted of a presentation on a particular topic related to the job search, I honestly can't remember what it was about, though I do remember one attendee who spoke up at the end.

"This is all fine and good, but it is pointless when you can't get past the HR Black Hole!"

The rest of the room murmured and nodded their agreement, so she went on: "I mean, you can't even get a personal response!" More murmuring and nodding of heads. I can't remember what the facilitator said, but it was little more than to go along with the herd. Oh how I wanted to speak up, but I couldn't, lest I give away my position and reason for being there.

So, I held my tongue. Until now.

First things first, the "HR Black Hole" she was referring to is actually called an Applicant Tracking System. If you are going to badmouth something, at least use its proper name. That being out of the way, why do we need these cursed Applicant Tracking Systems anyway? Why can't we as job seekers just send our resumes directly to recruiters and have them look at our obvious skill set and experience and send us along our rightful way to the hiring authority? To understand this, it is important that you understand a little history of this thing you might have heard of... the internet.

Once upon a time, if you wanted to apply for a job you had to mail your resume. By mail, I mean as in with a stamp. Stamps were, and relatively speaking still are, cheap, but they still cost something. For every resume you sent out, that was a letter you had to fold, an envelope you had to lick, and a stamp you had to stick on it. Having done all this, you then had to walk it to the mailbox and put it into a slot.

During this same time period, if you were a recruiter your best bet to advertise for jobs were in the newspaper. You've heard of those, right? If you wanted to post a job, you had to call up your representative at the newspaper several days before the day you wanted the ad to run, then fax (that's right, *fax*) your copy over. Then a month or so later you would get a bill, often for over $1,000, which was the going rate at the Houston Chronicle in the late '90s for a Sunday and Wednesday ad.

Then along came the internet and with it Monster and Hotjobs (these were the first two that I remember), and for recruiters, they were a dream. For one thing, a 30-day posting on Monster ran me a couple of hundred bucks, and I got three times the resumes within **hours** of posting the job. It was awesome! Except for one teeny little problem: while I was getting a lot more applications, I was also getting a lot more crap as well. For example, high school kids who tried to equate their experience counting down their tills at Kroger with what I was needing in a Corporate Controller.

For me, the reason was obvious: before online job boards, if you were an applicant you had to put a little skin in the game (as well as some saliva). With online job boards, you could apply for every job you saw in a matter of seconds. No printing, no buying stamps, no licking envelopes, no walking to the mailbox. Pre-Monster, if a stamp was $0.25, to apply for 200 jobs would run you $50, not to mention the time to stuff, lick, and mail the resumes. In the early days of job boards, you could apply for 200 jobs in 20 minutes and it wouldn't cost you a dime.

HR people can be slow on the uptake, but we did realize pretty early in that this simply wasn't going to work. As more people looked for work on the internet, the number of applications continued to grow. We loved the scale that the internet brought us, but the time spent wading through all those resumes was killing us. So out of this, the Applicant Tracking System was born.

So there you have it, the history behind the HR Black Hole. It is designed to make HR people's lives easier. Good for HR, bad for job applicants. But how do you get around it? A good place to start is to find people who might know someone at the place you are applying and be willing to put in a good word. The Applicant Tracking System makes resume and application retrieval fairly easy, so if your name gets mentioned by the right person, it can be pretty easy to have your file rise to the top. Another tip is to remember that it is a numbers game. Because applying for jobs takes less effort than the pre-ATS days, you are likely one of the hundreds, if not THOUSANDS of candidates vying for the same slot. It's hard, but don't get discouraged. Finally, it probably wouldn't hurt to apply for jobs where you are actually qualified. Have a good track record closing out your till at Kroger? That's fantastic, but don't be mad if you don't get a call for that CFO posting.

FAITH

Once upon a time, during a time Anthropologists collectively refer to as "The '80s," a certain singer made a solo album with a bunch of hit songs. The singer's name was George Michael, the album was "Faith," and the title track was one of those hits. I used to sing along with it when it played on MTV; imitating George Michael's moves, imagining that I too had a giant gold cross swaying from my ear and that I was wearing actual Ray-Ban Aviators and not a pair of five-dollar shades I bought at the local Stop-N-Go. For those of you who are perhaps of a younger generation. The MTV of yore used to play music videos - in fact, that is what the M stands for! You bought the book for the HR, but there's so much more!

Which brings me to this final chapter: Faith. This is going to get a little personal, and frankly, it might even turn some readers off, but I have to get it out there. You've made it this far, you can do one more chapter, right?

Not too long ago I found myself in a place that few people want to be in: searching for full-time work. I was fortunate in that I knew the change was coming, which was nice, but that isn't to say I wasn't concerned because let's face it, while I enjoy writing, I'm not ready to quit my day job. I do know people whose sole occupation is blogging, but they also live with their parents and conveniently "forget" their wallets every time we meet for lunch.

When I first learned that I would be needing to make a change, I found myself having some pretty regular conversations with God, to the point that I think He was getting tired of hearing from me.

I asked for the right job: one that He wanted me in, one where I could do the most good as defined by Him, but I also threw in one minor, personal, selfish request as well - that I would have a job before I left my previous employer.

One day, about 3 weeks into this new adventure, I was walking the dog and praying (pleading, really). As I walked, prayed, and wondered if I had brought enough poop bags, I felt a sense of calm - a feeling in my bones - that He would answer this prayer. I was going to have a job before leaving my other one. After this experience, and it really was an experience, I felt better.

For a while.

Then, with a little less than a week before the big day, I started to have doubts.

A lot of doubts.

Maybe I hadn't heard from God, but rather I had heard from that afternoon's burrito, or maybe I just heard what I wanted to hear. Maybe, maybe, maybe... Then I was reminded of what has now become my personal mission statement: Proverbs 3:5&6, which reads "Trust in the Lord with all your heart and lean not on your own understanding; in all your ways acknowledge Him, and He will make your paths straight." As I read and re-read those verses, I was taken back to Jesus telling us that if we only have the faith of a mustard seed, we can move mountains. It is easy to read, and even believe at a core level, but actually practicing faith - practicing trusting God with ALL your heart - that's a whole other can of worms. Let me be super clear here, I didn't become a model of faith, no mountains were moved, but when I faced that fear and doubt I would remind myself that I just had to have faith.

And then the day came. I had my exit interview, carried out what few personal belongings I hadn't carted off the days before, and left for an interview in another town. As I drove home, I continued to remind myself that I truly did believe that God had spoken to me in a small, still, voice while on that walk, and that all I needed was to have faith and I would have a job before the end of the day.

And I kept reminding myself of this. Even as I looked at the clock in the car and wondered if perhaps God wasn't on Central Standard Time (which is crazy, I know. Texas is CST, so heaven must be as well).

I got home a few minutes before 5 and did the best I could to push back those doubts. Then the phone rang and the perfect opportunity for me right then was on the other end.

So, if you find yourself in the same boat, just remember the immortal words of George Michael: "I just gotta have faith, mmmm, I gotta have faith..."

ACKNOWLEDGEMENTS

This book, and the blog from hence it came, would not be possible were it not for the undying love and support of my wife, Kerri Perkins. She is my hope, inspiration, muse, and editor - reading drafts of almost all posts when she could be doing something more productive - like watching television. Her wisdom and candid feedback, such as "I don't get it," and "sorry, but that joke just isn't funny," is always appreciated.

The Thursday 'sghetti crew, particularly Mike, was instrumental in my moving forward with this project, though he didn't have a clue. Not only is he an inspiration for at least one (positive) example here, but he has politely informed me of typos from time to time. His, and all my Greek Spaghetti eating friends' moral support has always been appreciated more than they know. Chocolate cake is on me next time.

And, of course, all the readers of the blog. I couldn't have done it without either of you.

-Jim